Breathing
and Living Wall

ARTPOWER

Breathing and Living Wall
Copyright © Artpower International Publishing Co., Ltd.

ARTPOWER™

Designer: Chen Ting
Chief Editor: Weng Danzhi

Address: Room C, 9/F., Sun House, 181 Des Voeux Road Central,
Hong Kong, China
Tel: 852-31840676
Fax: 852-25432396

Editorial Department
Address: G009, Floor 7th, Yimao Centre, Meiyuan Road, Luohu District,
Shenzhen, China
Tel: 86-755-82913355
Fax: 86-755-82020029

Web: www.artpower.com.cn
E-mail: artpower@artpower.com.cn

ISBN 978-988-19973-6-4

Printed in China

PREFACE

The Vertical Gardens are here to stay, but it is very important to propose them from knowledge of plants and their physiological requirements and the different gradients that might be present in the same place.

The wonderful paradox of a future that is back to something primal, makes us dream; the life surrounded by plants. Fortunately, we, the human species, simian that inhabit the human ecosystem, are realizing the obvious, that our lives are empty and absurd if we aren't surrounded by nature. And for this, the new revolution, the eco-revolution, does not conceive full life in the asepsis of being girded by bare walls in the vortex of the most brutal consumerism.

In this wonderful edition of *Breathing and Living Wall*, is shown in color some of the more relevant projects worldwide, in which the eco-revolutionaries have given their all in their projects. Some of them are really complex in its execution and very thoughtful, some other are simpler and delightful and even some are ephemeral.

One might say then, that special attention should be paid to the experience of the specialists and no least important to the system to be used for every occasion. Not only we have to see how nice they seem once completed, but also the time those systems will secure the life they carry, and the respect and knowledge that the expert must put along with their demonstrable experience in their technique to make the project viable.

There is however one crucial point to be taken very seriously, we have to be very careful with the failures, because it affects everyone; the ones that developed the system, the architect of the property and even the introduction of the vertical gardens in future projects. This is why everyone must be very clear that the price and the ones which struggles for who is the cheapest, are swampy and full of traps in small prints, that hinders the path of success for Vertical Gardens. Either way, it is always valuable to incorporate these systems into our gray cities environment considering the above.

I trust in the potential to include green design elements, which is why architects and designers should be ahead and share our vision. It is true that in the embodiment of vertical gardens, the design, the artistic and functionality are the basics; but perhaps, solely seeing in that way, might prove to be selfish. It is the job of the inhabitants of this world, unfortunately individualist, to become aware in making available the nature to the rest of his kind, popularizing and making the Living Walls accessible and not elitist. It would be absurd that only have green design in the high profile buildings; in the same way that we found abhorrent any social difference; but disastrously, they exist.

Thankfully, nature is back, as long as we allow it; indeed there is much to do, and Vertical Gardens are not the magical cure to the ills that plague the planet or anything, but it's a tiny bit in the right path and above all, the opportunity to reflect, refresh and envision the future standing in front of some of the wonders that are present in *Breathing and Living Wall*.

Each and every one of us has the opportunity to leave a trace; the fact that we inherited a sick world does not give us the right to handing it over to the future generations.

Ignacio Solano Cabello
Founding director of Paisajismo Urbano
Developer of the Vertical Ecosystem

CONTENTS

002 Chamber of Commerce and Industry

006 House in Travessa Do Patrocínio

008 IDEO Morph 38

010 Casa CorManca

014 Quai Branly Museum

016 Modera Hotel

018 Heineken House

022 CAVA Restaurant, Wine Bar

024 Natural Systems Domination

028 Illura Apartments

030 The Block Sky High TV Series

032 Greenery in Paris

034 Jules and Jim Hotel

036 Grow

038 Stacking Green

040 Stone House

042 Caixa Forum Madrid

044 Google Campus

046 Airbnb Headquarters

048 Foundation for the Carolinas

050 Athenaeum Hotel

052 Ocean Financial Centre

054 1 Bligh Street

056 Pont Juvénal

058 Alpha Park

060 Trussardi Cafe

062 ITE Headquarters and ITE College Central

066 L'Oasis D'Aboukir

068 La Maison-vague

070 Vertical Garden in Quito Shopping Mall

072 Hotel B3 Vertical Garden

074 Louis Vuitton

076 Contemporary Logement Loft

078 Dutch Energy Company Eneco's New Rotterdam Headquarters

081	Park Royal on Pickering	126	EL JAPONEZ CDA Restaurant
086	SmogShoppe	128	EL JAPONEZ Restaurant
090	Triptych Apartments	130	Vertical Garden in Replay Store, Florence
092	Green Roofing Tile Cabin	131	Vertical Garden in Replay Store, Paris
094	Unique Lounge	132	Babylone Pendant
099	The Vegetal Abacus	134	Moving Hedge Room Divider
100	Ideal Hotel	136	Plantwalls
102	Green Symphony et Public au Taipei Concert Hall	140	Nike Sportswear Store
104	Sultan Ibrahim	144	Tori Tori Restaurant
106	Sweet Tea	146	Café Banka
110	Amazonia at the Heart of Restaurant	148	New York Botanical Garden
112	Corsairfly	150	Freehills Offices
114	Montreuil Showroom	152	Mahogany Room in Crown Casino
116	NS House	154	Indoor Vertical Garden Luxury Villa in Ibiza
120	Vertical Garden in Replay Store, Barcelona	156	Indoor Vertical Garden Poncelet Cheese Bar in Madrid
122	Vertical Garden in Replay Store, Milan	158	Indoor Vertical Garden SPA Hotel Castle Son Claret
124	Downtown Hotel	160	Mini-Farmery

162 72 and Sunny

164 Barbara Bestor Residence

166 Snog Productions

168 Karoo

170 Capitaland, Six Battery Road, Rainforest Rhapsody

172 Capitol Clothing Shop

173 Juvia Restaurant

174 8 Napier Road

179 158 Cecil Street

182 Miami Art Museum

184 Amazonica Floresta

186 San Diego Vertical Garden

190 Home 06

192 GLOBAL WORK et.

194 Furstadtskaya Street Maternity Hospital

198 Intensivnik

200 "Neskuchnyi Sad" Restaurant

202 NVIDIA

204 The Living Wall with Plant and Stone

206 Pushkin

210 Vodokanal

212 Yanino

216 Rustic Canyon Residence

218 Tinga Restaurant

220 Vertical Garden Penthouse in Murcia

222 Moss Your City

224 Rommen

226 ION Orchard and The Orchard Residences

228 The Coast at Sentosa Cove

230 Albizzia House

232 Nature Individuelle

234 KKCG

238 MEGAFON Retail Store

242 Contributors

Chamber of Commerce and Industry

Design Agency
Chartier-Corbasson Architectes

Client
CCI de Picardie

Location
Amiens, France

Area
1, 800 m²

Photography
R. Meffre & Y. Marchand

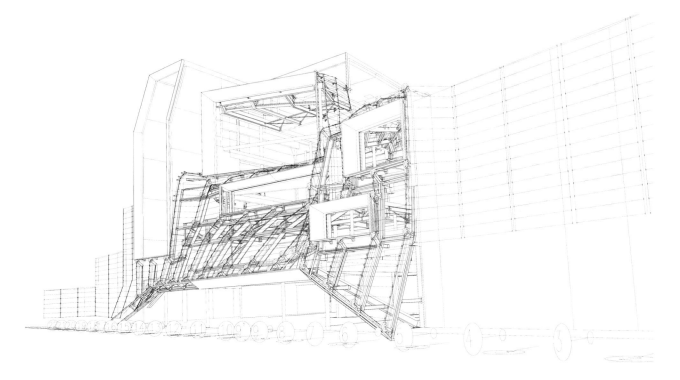

The Bouctot-Vagniez Town Hall in Amiens is a remarkable building, an architectural testament to the glories of Art Nouveau in nineteen-twenties. Our project is concerned with designing an extension to this unique building, which is home to the Picardy Regional Chamber of Commerce and Industry.

All the essential features of the project are represented in a plinth of living greenery that creates a link between the new wing, the existing premises and the gardens. The offices will be situated above this greenery plinth. They are housed in two separate spaces divided from one another by an atrium that will allow natural light and air to penetrate

the heart of the building. Screen-printing technology protects certain perspectives by shading the glazed areas or leaving them clear, according to the needs created by the utilisation of the rooms behind. To the south, on the roadside elevation, a double skin of metal mesh allows for ventilation and creates a sunscreen, creating a secluded atmosphere in the offices.

As regards the garden elevation, the design forms part of the existing landscaping as a sort of kink in the boundary wall. The hall opens out as broadly as possible onto the gardens, and the ground floor rises up to embrace a wide panoramic bay window creating a fluid, light-filled space.

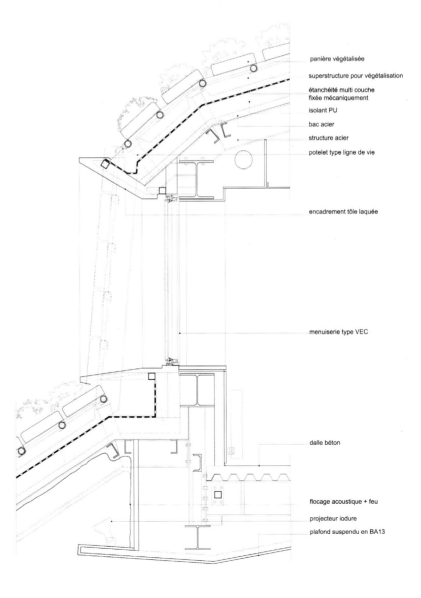

panière végétalisée

superstructure pour végétalisation

étanchéité multi couche
fixée mécaniquement

isolant PU

bac acier

structure acier

potelet type ligne de vie

encadrement tôle laquée

menuiserie type VEC

dalle béton

flocage acoustique + feu

projecteur iodure

plafond suspendu en BA13

House in Travessa Do Patrocínio

Design Agency
RA \\ ARCHITECTURAL & DESIGN STUDIO

Architects
Luís Rebelo de Andrade, Tiago Rebelo de Andrade & Manuel Cachão Tojal

Co-Workers
Madalena Rebelo de Andrade, Raquel Jorge, Carlos Ruas & Tiago Moniz

Client
BWA — Buildings With Art

Location
Lisbon, Portugal

Area
248 m²

Photography
FG+SG — Fernando Guerra, Sergio Guerra

From a small lot with it's unique implantation, this project has raised early on a couple of challenges... and along with them, ideas emerged.

The box housing deviates from the gable to create a vertical yard (glass box), with a straight ladder connecting all floors, an allusion to the famous stairs of Alfama, running between the all 4 floors walls and linking the various dimensions.

This courtyard is the heart of the house, bringing light to the interior, enhancing the main entrance and creating a real exterior/interior relationship.

In terms of material, we chose to polish the rectangular form and gave the block the face of a tree, making it one more element of the square, which resulted together with the existing tree and water fountain, in a triad.

The program was set up almost automatically, the technical services and garage with direct access from the street. The first floor holds the private area of the house, the second floor is the social area,

with a direct connection to the coverage, extending social into outdoors, being the view related to the social side and the private area to both square and embassy, the setting of a typical Lisbon experience, which is a truly intimate relationship between quarters.

Therefore, this project is in fact a mini lung and

an example of sustainability for the city of Lisbon, keeping the principles of a living typical habitat and a relationship with the outside, assuming a revitalizing urban role.

Its walls are completely covered with vegetation, creating a vertical garden, filled with around 4, 500 plants from 25 different Iberian and Mediterranean

varieties which occupies 100 square meters. So, short levels of water consumption are guaranteed as well as little gardening challenges. Different fragrance are spread throughout the 4 floors. For example, in the swimming pool you will have the flavor of saffron, in the bedroom, lavender, in the living-room, rosemary.

Implemented in the heart of a busy city, the vertical garden creates a unique link with nature and an unexpected atmosphere.

IDEO Morph 38

Design Agency	Designer	Landscape Architect
Somdoon Architects	Punpong Wiwatkul, Puiphai Khunawat	Shma Company Limited
Location	**Area**	**Photography**
Bangkok, Thailand	3,102 m²	W Workspace, Somdoon Architects

The scheme is located away from the high density and congestion of Sukhumvit road and into a blissfully green low-rise residential area. The development has been separated into two towers to maximize plot ratio, and each building targets to different potential tenants in character.

The two towers are visually interconnected through a folding "Tree Bark" envelope that wraps around from the 32-storey rear tower (Ashton) and 10 duplex-storey front tower (Skyle). This outer skin is a combination of precast concrete panels, expanded meshes and planters. The functions of the skin varies from being sun shading devices to covering air condensing units. The bark on the west and east side strategically becomes green walls, in accordance to the tropic sun's orientation. The height of this wall is 65 m on the front tower and 130 m on the rear tower respectively, providing the residences and neighbors with a comfortable visual and natural environment.

Skyle is targeted for singles or young couples with the smallest unit footprint being 23.3 m². These duplex units are expressed vertically with variation of balconies and air condensing units.

In contrast, Ashton emphasizes on the horizontal and cantilevered spaces which are targeted to families. The units' sizes and types vary from a single bed with a reading room, to duplex units with a private swimming pool and a garden on the 8th floor, and a four bed duplex penthouse at top level. A 2.4-m cantilevered living space projects from each unit on the North side. This is made up of a glazing enclosure on three sides providing the maximum view. Each unit on the south has a semi-outdoor balcony which is flexible in space. The double layer of sliding windows allow for a transition between a conventional balcony to an extended indoor living area.

The IDEO Morph 38 is a high rise building which is located in stark contrast to the low-rise residential context. The project takes on a symbiotic relationship with the environment. Due to its sensitive design language and the green populated facade, the buildings have a natural aesthetic, making them a landmark and a pleasant environment for the neighbors and the city.

Casa CorManca

Design Agency
PAUL CREMOUX Studio

Architect
Paul Cremoux W.

Location
Mexico

Photography
Héctor Armanado Herrera and
Paul Cremoux Wanderstok

2012 — 2013, on a 12 meters by 13 meters (39 feet by 42 feet) plot of land, a monolithic volume is transformed in order to attain luminous indoor spaces. Slade stone at the exterior facades is contrasted with the soft beech like wood finish, achieving great definition and space discovery.

Built in a small plot of land 174 m^2 (1, 872 square feet), the construction rises looking south to the vertical vegetation garden wall. It is a 3 stories high assembly where the main terrace is to be found at the second level, following by a small lecture studio.

This area is intent to transform radically the notion of "open patio garden" since there is not really space to ensure a ground courtyard, the main terrace plays a social definitive role.

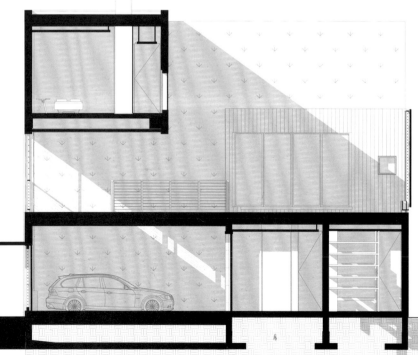

Recyclable content materials, VOC paint, cross ventilations highly used and passive energy-temperature control strategies are bound into the core design. Three heat exhaustion chimney work as main devices to control hot temperature at bedrooms areas.

Vertical garden is a major air quality and humidity creator, where before there wasn't any plant, now we have planted over 4, 000 (absorbing 267kg of CO_2 per year).

We would like to think about vegetation not only as a practical temperature, humidity and comfort control device, or as a beautiful energetic view, but also as an element that acts like a light curtain, accomplishing the idea of a theatrical dramatic plane, where more space is to be found at the back.

Quai Branly Museum

Designer
Patrick Blanc

Architect
Jean Nouvel

This project designed by Patrick Blanc, is one of the finest gardening fantasy in French.

The vegetal wall at the Quai Branly museum faces north, protecting it from brutal sunlight which undoubtedly poses a serious challenge to these vertical plantings, especially in summer.

Modera Hotel

Designer
Lango Hansen Landscape Architects

Client
Posh Ventures, LLC

Location
Portland, Oregon

The outdated motor-court of a 1960's Era motel has been reborn as a vibrant social space that is a distillation of the verdant Pacific Northwest landscape. Located on the newly redesigned transportation mall in downtown Portland, hotel guests, restaurant patrons, and even curious passersby enjoy this urban oasis.

The reclaimed courtyard, featuring a living wall, wood screens and outdoor fire pits, is now the anchor for a restaurant and the completely renovated boutique hotel. The 19.5 m (64 feet) long living wall is a focal point of the lush courtyard and is a pixilated abstraction of the Pacific Northwest itself, with its weathered steel panels alluding to outcroppings of basalt set within the rich textures of the forest.

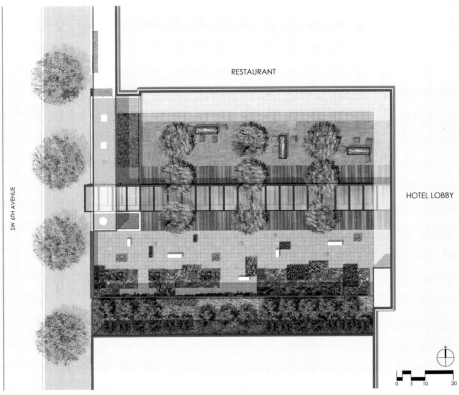

RESTAURANT

SW 6TH AVENUE

HOTEL LOBBY

0 5 10 20

Heineken House

HEINEKEN HOUSE

Design Agency
Art Arquitectos S.C.

Location
Polanco, Mexico

Area
1, 300 m²

Photography
Paul Czitrom / Marisol Paredes

The project for the Heineken bar and corporate offices of Cuauhtémoc Moctezuma Heineken Mexico located in a big house in the Polanco area of Mexico City — catalogued as historic patrimony by INBA — was selected through a competition organized by the client.

It was very important that the original and main architectonics features of the residence were preserved and at the same time incorporated in a very contemporary trend, the brand image by creating the office areas and the Bar House for special guests and tastings.

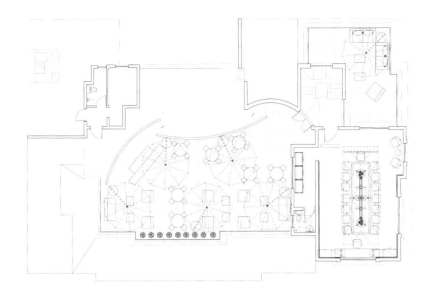

CAVA Restaurant, Wine Bar

Design Agency
Charles C. Hugo Landscape Design

An integrated drip system and picking the right plants for the site conditions have been key components of this wall's success. Charles C. Hugo Landscape Design were excited to create the public art display that was new and cutting edge for the Seacoast.

Natural Systems Domination

Design Agency	Principal Designer	Location	Photography
tres birds workshop	Mike Moore	Denver, US	Kristin Glenn

Domination implies taking over. If we had it our way, natural systems would dominate entirely. Natural systems operate in perfect efficiency. Humans are both part of those natural systems and also somehow separate (by choice). The further we stray from connections with nature, the more alien we become. tres birds workshop was commissioned to concept, design and build an art installation in Downtown Denver for the purpose of encouraging people out of their offices for daily fresh air breaks. We highly recommend it. The installation made up of part vintage office furniture and part

100% live vegetation reminds us not to let office overgrowth affect a healthy relationship with the outdoors. All of the vegetation used in the installation were reused and recycled afterward.

tres birds workshop does more with less and is a leader in creating unique design experiences as well as custom environments that align with individual client lifestyles, workflows and desires. tres birds workshop considers lowering embodied energy,

increasing use of natural day light and facilitating connections between humans and the natural environment top priorities in architecture. The process of any tres birds workshop project is interdisciplinary, combining knowledge from art, science, anthropology, architecture and construction. tres birds workshop seeks collaborative solutions to building challenges in order to affect both people and the planet in positive ways.

Illura Apartments

Vertical Garden Constructor
Fytogreen

Architect
Elenberg Fraser Architects

Landscape Architect
Tract

Location
West Melbourne

Area
121 m²

As a street view of a modern apartment block in an old part of inner Melbourne, the vertical garden makes a powerful impact.

Made up of a series of 4 elevated sections with the gardens facing North East, these will need to tolerate full sun in summer.

The architecture and the vertical gardens complement each other to create a modern and fresh look for the 3 level apartments. Using strappy foliage and also flat growing ground covering plants, the textural elements will last as the garden evolves over time.

The Block Sky High TV Series

Vertical Garden Constructor
Fytogreen

Architect
Julian Brenchley Architects

Client
The Block Sky High TV Series for
Channel 9

Location
South Melbourne

Area
117 m²

Outdoor vertical gardens installed on all 4 aspects of the tower block. The vertical gardens are in 25 sections spread over level 1 to 5. Contrasting with a Black steel surrounded, the green foliage will develop over time to be a sustainable evergreen look with some flowering species creating seasonal highlights.

Greenery in Paris

Design Agency	Location	Area
Jardins de Babylone	Paris, France	12.5 m²

This green wall creates a link between the two parts of the garden and access to the stairs and the kitchen. Rounded, it reduces the building's corners and provides freshness in summer.

The choice of plants was made on alternating blooms throughout the seasons and foliage perennials and shrubs.

Jules and Jim Hotel

Design Agency
Jardins de Babylone

Location
Paris, France

Area
45 m²

The initial idea of this project was to bring the plant rather than mineral in the two paved courtyard of the Jules and Jim Hotel.

The only constraint we had was to offer the customer a plant palette of foliage in shades of green with a low development and to create a more serene plant design and atmosphere in this enclosed space.

At the completion of the second plant wall in the next yard, we took the idea of wave Helxine to create continuity in the design of the plant wall. Plant palette has worked with the same concept as the first green wall.

Grow

Designer
SpY

Partly pruned climber formed
a circle on a wall. The main
branches were saved to ensure
new growth.

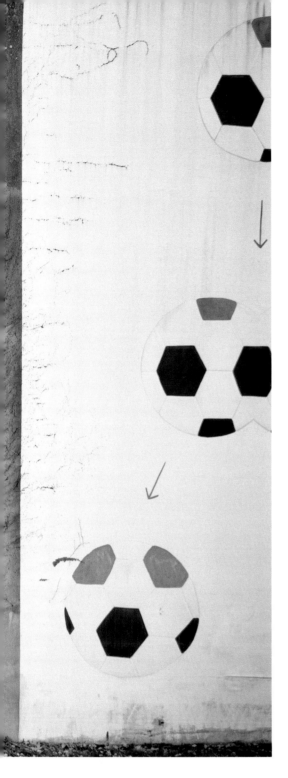

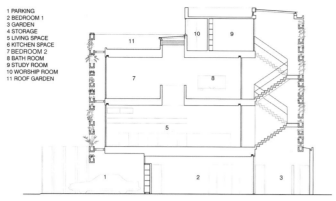

1 PARKING
2 BEDROOM 1
3 GARDEN
4 STORAGE
5 LIVING SPACE
6 KITCHEN SPACE
7 BEDROOM 2
8 BATH ROOM
9 STUDY ROOM
10 WORSHIP ROOM
11 ROOF GARDEN

Elevation S:1/150

Section S:1/150

Stacking Green

Design Agency
Vo Trong Nghia Architects

Principal Architects
Vo Trong Nghia, Daisuke Sanuki,
Shunri Nishizawa (3 principals)

Contractor
Wind and Water House JSC

Location
Ho Chi Minh City (Saigon), Vietnam

Area
215 m²

Photography
Hiroyuki Oki

The house is a very typical tube house constructed on the plot 4m wide and 20m deep. The front and back facades are entirely composed of layers of concrete planters cantilevered from two sidewalls, inspired by the Saigonese culture of displaying green on private houses. We named this tropical, unique and green house as Stacking Green because its facades were filled with vigorous and vital greenery. The green facade and roof top garden protect its inhabitants from the direct sunlight, street noise and pollution. Furthermore, natural ventilation through the facades and 2 skylights allow this house to save a huge amount of energy in a harsh climate in Saigon. Concerning these ecological approaches, we referred a lot to the bioclimatic principles of traditional Vietnamese courtyard house.

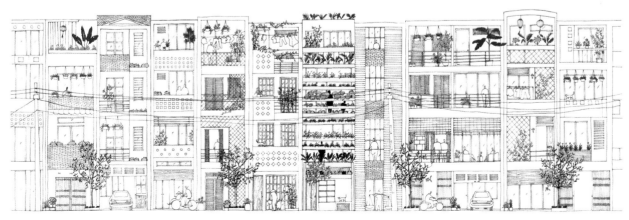

Stone House

Design Agency
Vo Trong Nghia Architects

Principal Architects
Vo Trong Nghia

Contractor
Wind and Water House JSC

Location
Vietnam

Area
360 m²

Photography
Hiroyuki Oki

This torus-shaped stone house is located in a quiet residential quarter en route from Hanoi to Ha Long Bay. A rising green roof and walls composed of subdued dark blue stones create a landscape, which stands out boldly in the new residential area.

The rooms surround the oval courtyard, making a colony-like relationship with each other. Circulating flow runs around the courtyard and continues to the green roof, connecting all places in the house. This courtyard and green roof compose a sequential garden, which creates a rich relationship between inside and outside the house. Residents experience the changes of the seasons and learn to appreciate their wealthy life with nature, thanks to this sequential garden.

To create a wall with smooth curvature, cubic stones with a thickness of 10cm were carefully stacked. Consequently, the wall performs the play of light and shadow. Massive and meticulous texture of the wall generates a cave-like space, which recalls the image of a primitive house.

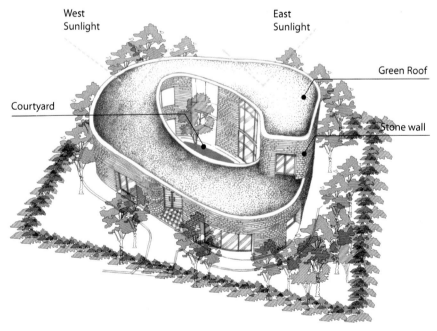

West Sunlight

East Sunlight

Green Roof

Courtyard

Stone wall

Axonometric Diagram

Caixa Forum Madrid

Designer
Patrick Blanc

Architect
Herzog & de Meuron

Location
Madird, Spain

The vertical garden of the Caixa Forum Madrid is not only the first to be installed in Spain but also the largest implemented to date on a facade without gaps, as it has a planted surface area of 460 m². The result is a surprising, multicoloured "living painting", in addition to being visually attractive, also acts as an effective environmental agent. The vertical garden forms an impressive natural tapestry made up of 15,000 plants of 250 different species that have transformed one of the buildings adjoining the developed area of the Caixa Forum Madrid into a surprising garden. The wall covers the entirety of the adjoining building at the edge of the new public square that provides access, from Paseo del Prado, to the Caixa Forum Madrid at its northern end; in other words, the wall next to number 34 Paseo del Prado.

Google Campus

Designer
Wayward Plants

Location
London, UK

Wayward Plants designed and built the Living Technologies Garden in the new Google Campus London, a unique co-working space in the heart of East London's Tech City which supports tech start-ups.

A handmade moss wall wraps the courtyard, utilizing an innovative rainwater collection system. The gaps in the walls are tagged with Moss Graffiti, a guerrilla gardening tactic. Woodland planting of ferns and hellebores fill the concrete planters in this shady space.

Plant Thirst Detectors, which can be found throughout the garden, were designed by Technology Will Save Us, a haberdashery for technology and education. These were originally developed in response to Wayward Plants' Urban Physic Garden 2011.

The Living Technology Garden will facilitate ongoing collaborations with start-ups that merges plants and technology.

Airbnb Headquarters

Design Agency	Architect	Client	Location	Photograpghy
Meyer + Silberberg Land Architects	Gensler	SKS Investment	San Francisco, US	Drew Kelly

Meyer + Silberberg teamed with Gensler and SKS to reinvigorate the Jewelry Gift Center and adjacent office buildings in San Francisc's SOMA district. As part of the restoration of these historic buildings, the existing loading dock was converted into elevated plaza, connecting the Jewelry Center to the adjoining newly renovated office building. Built around an imported specimen maple tree on axis with the office atrium, an elevated wooden plaza floats above the old loading dock entry. A ring of "semi-precious stones" adorns the tree, distinguishes the courtyard, and provides a sheltered social place for tenants to wait, nibble or read. Other components include a wall of succulents concealing a utility corridor, and a fern-lined lounging/work platform.

Foundation for the Carolinas

Designer
Patrick Blanc

Location
Charlotte NC, US

This beautiful vertical garden designed by Patrick Blanc is located in Charlotte NC.

Athenaeum Hotel

Designer
Patrick Blanc

Location
London, UK

The eight-storey green wall is located in London's Athenaeum Hotel. Patrick Blanc, a French botanist, designed the wall, which includes 260 species and 12,000 actual plants.

Ocean Financial Centre

Design Agency	Location	Area
Tierra Design (S) Pte Ltd.	Singapore	6,109 m²

The tropical gardens in the sky at the Ocean Financial Centre were designed within the interstitial spaces between the building structure and facade framing. Creating a connection to the natural environment, the vertical landscaping at the highest floors from the 39th to the 43rd level provides a lush setting. These areas provide much needed relaxation and relief to users who spend most of their time in the artificially ventilated environment of an office building. In response to the hard surface of the structural framing of the building, the landscaping provides a contrasting effect softening the lines and creating an intimate experience. The canopy trees at the 41st floor create an interesting play of scale and different textures and colours of plantings offer a vibrant visual treat.

The vertical green frames are comprised of planters located at every 1.5m. The lightweight mesh structure is planted with fast growing Thunbergia grandiflora climber species to ensure a full green cover. The colourful purple flowers and the large leaf foliage add to the tropical feel of the interactive garden space. A combination of profuse flowering plants and colourful textured leaf foliage of shrubs at the base of the green columns lends an exciting and vibrant feel to this limited landscape space. At the 43rd level, the green columns are combined with a horizontal trellis feature to create a green arbor in the sky. Horizontal planter trays at regular intervals planted with trailing plants to cover the trellis and form a soft green canopy for the sky garden users.

A series of tropical garden views, outdoor walks and seating at different levels create a work environment that is refreshing and unique. The landscaping within the interstitial spaces between the building structure and the facade framing blurs the boundary between the building and the natural environment.

1 Bligh Street

Vertical Garden Constructor	Architect	Client	Location	Area
Fytogreen	Architectus & Ingenhoven	Dexus Property Group	Sydney, Australia	377 m^2

"Beautiful, bold and brilliantly green" is the way that this next generation sustainable office building is described. The 27-level tower at 1 Bligh Street is Sydney's latest 6-Star Green Star Office Design V2 Certified building which promises to provide a new benchmark in sustainable design.

Fytogreen created a 377 m^2 green wall. The wall required shade and wind tolerant plant species and was specified by the architect to be "uniform green", with "simplicity rather than Celebration" as its theme. The 40 metre long green wall presents its own site challenges due to its solar orientation.

A research and development program will support the ongoing maintenance of the green wall. As this vertical garden approaches its third birthday it is still Australia's largest single vertical garden that is Ecologically Sustainable.

Pont Juvénal

Designer

Patrick Blanc

A huge living wall stand by the road, being a great view. The posh and bright greenery of the large plantwall is very compact and manageable.

Alpha Park

Designer
Patrick Blanc

Location
Paris, France

The project is the largest vertical garden in the World — 2, 000 m² of vegetal facade.

Trussardi Cafe

Architect
Carlo Ratti Associati

Vertical Garden Consultant
Patrick Blanc

Client
Trussardi s.p.a.

Area
60 m^2

The proposed extension of the Trussardi Cafe through a closed terrace, in the French style, follows a study of new functions for the ground floor of the headquarters of the fashion house in Piazza della Scala, Milan. The new terrace acts as a glass case with a real hanging garden suspended from the roof, made possible thanks to the "green wall" invented by the French botanist Patrick Blanc. More than 120 different plant species are placed on the thin support structure, creating the effect of a green cloud floating in space. In addition to the visual effect, 100 square meters of plant-life are brought into the square without taking up floor space, improving air quality and providing shade during the summer season. With the use of a living element as the building material the entire structure can be interpreted as an organism with its own metabolism.

ITE Headquarters and ITE College Central

Design Agency
RSP Architects Planners &
Engineers (Pte) Ltd.

Location
2 Ang Mo Kio Drive, Singapore

Client
Institute of Technical Education

ITE Headquarters and ITE College Central is the third ITE Regional Campus Development to be completed as part of the Government's plan to develop ITE as a world class Technical Education Institution. ITE endeavors to be exemplary of good building design while promoting environmental consciousness through innovative design of this new campus.

The overall Green Strategy is the creation of an assimilation of the green environment with the various building blocks, through weaving the green "fingers" with the main activity spaces within the campus, providing natural greenery to every blocks. A major thoroughfare is introduced throughout the main spine of the campus, where students meet and interact. This Central Green Spine also known as Inspiration Spine catches the prevailing wind with its primary axis in the north-south orientation, enabling the various blocks to be

effectively cross-ventilated and therefore reduces the need for mechanical ventilation.

The overall landscape plan is defined by two distinctive planting characters, Boundary Planting and Central Green Spine. The Boundary Planting, an interface with the surrounding land and city

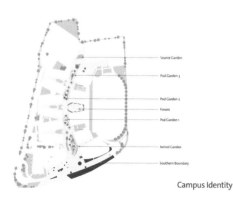

Campus Identity

is defined by a layered plant matrix to simulate native Singaporean rain-forest. The diversity of the plant species will provide a balanced ecosystem.

The Inspiration Spine is defined by a series of themed gardens to enhance the users' experience, aid orientation and create a unique collective identity for the campus. These themed gardens will concentrate on the perception of the planting from below (Ground level/E-deck/Building surrounding) and from above (Roof Garden/Green Terrace), which together, give the campus a unique 3-dimensional character and showcase the extensive planting pallet.

Another distinctive aspect of this development is the extensive use of Green Wall on the west-facing facades of the school and workshop blocks. The Green Wall not only acts as natural sun-shading components to improve the micro-climate indoors but also provides a key recognisable design feature to ITE Headquarters and ITE College Central, adding colour and nature to complement the overall design. These vertical greening cooling measures largely reduce thermal heat gain and create a more comfortable and user-friendly environment

Spine Isometric

PLANTS IMAGE

for the users. The 5, 600 m^2 Green Wall provided is one of the largest in the world for a single development.

All planting provided in the development is to positively improve the micro-climate, to provide shelter for the intermediate spaces, to create shade and to enhance wildlife habitat as well as provide visual delight.

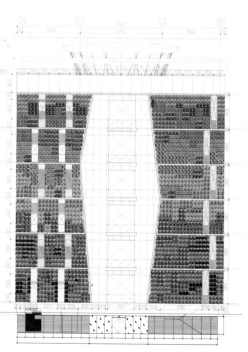

BLOCK- D WEST ELEVATION
SCALE 1:100

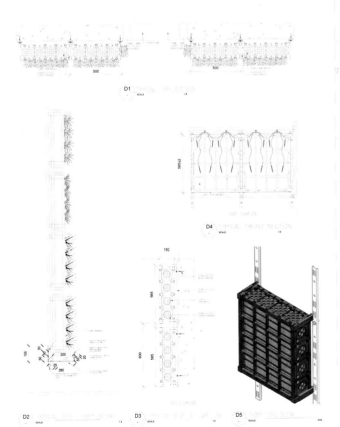

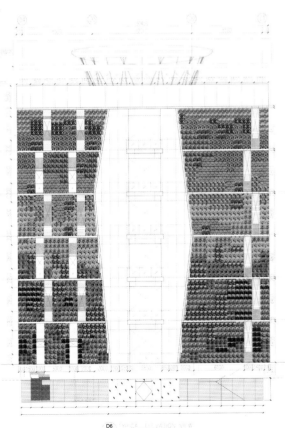

L'Oasis D'Aboukir

Designer
Patrick Blanc

Location
Paris, France

L'Oasis D'Aboukir is a project completed by Patrick Blanc and located in Paris, France.

The vertical garden decorates the facade of a historic building in the heart of the city, and features 7, 600 plants from 237 different species.

LE MIRAGE VERT
- Rue d'Aboukir - PARIS

La Maison-vague

Design Agency
mlapresse

Designer
Patrick Nadeau

Client
Effort Rémois

Location
Sillery, France

Area
110 m²

La Maison-vague uses vegetation for its architectural and environmental qualities, particularly in terms of thermal insulation. A fully vegetated shell protects the interior from summer heat and winter cold. The basic form is to encapsulate within a single mat of vegetation that undulates and floats above the ground. The traditional relationship between house and garden is changed, disturbed even, the project encompasses both in the same construction.

The vegetation has been designed with Pierre Georgel (Ecovégétal). The house is covered with soil that mimics that of a natural slope. The technical challenge lay primarily in the steep slope that required the development of innovative systems for the maintenance of land and water retention.

The plants were selected for their aesthetic qualities and their ability to adapt to the environment (resistance over time and minimal maintenance). It is a mix of sedums, grasses, thyme, lavender and other perennials and small aromatic herbs that are distributed according to the inclination of the hull. An automatic watering system is provided but it is only reserved for periods of very severe drought.

The house is alive, changing its appearance, color and odor with the seasons. New plants can be brought by the wind, insects or birds and give the building a certain character or even a fallow ground-wave, hence the name La Maison-vague, which could equally and poetically signify an ocean wave or an open field (terrain vague).

Vertical Garden in Quito Shopping Mall

Design Agency
Paisajismo Urbano

Location
Ecuador

In October 2012, the designers completed the American continent's largest vertical garden in Ecuador in a record time of one and a half month.

This is a vertical ecosystem of 1, 000 m² divided into 9 vertical gardens surrounding a shopping center in Quito.

Paisajismo Urbano has been made to this building both outdoor and indoor vertical gardens. 30, 000 plants were planted from 90 different species. Among them, 60 species are native, preceded by a thorough investigation into the rainforests of Iasuní.

Paisajismo Urbano has chosen this project for bio-architecture, which in a year will generate oxygen for 1, 000 people and catch 300 tons of harmful gases, creating a relaxed and unique environment for leisure.

Hotel B3 Vertical Garden

Design Agency
Paisajismo Urbano

Location
Colombia

One of the largest gardens in South America is four hundred square meters holding 25,000 plants from over 60 families, most of them are native. It has been a labor of species selection made following an investigation in Colombian rainforests, which has resulted in the most emblematic Vertical Garden in Bogotá.

This magnificent vertical garden has been made in 2012 in partnership with our new partners and distributors, the company GRONCOL in Bogotá, Colombia. This vertical ecosystem has become a landmark in the city and a seal for its owners, owners of the most original hotel in Colombia.

Louis Vuitton

Designer	Client	Location	Photography
mlapresse	Patrick Nadeau	Paris, France	Colin Sayetta

The plan of terrace is organized into two large areas:

The esplanade is an open area situated near the entrance. It is a transformable space devoted to events and exhibitions. Essentially composed of several small, mobile gardens — it is an evocation of the voyage tradition and the travel trunks intrinsically associated with the company vision of Louis Vuitton. This space reminds us that plants, like people, also travel. Whether a result of natural occurrence will be brought along from one place to the next by human activity, plants forever circulate from one continent to the next.

The wood is an intimate space reserved for meetings and individual appointments. It is composed of meeting table nested amidst trees. These trees are planted in large leather and textile bags inspired by the sacks traditionally used to protect roots and earth in the transport of vegetation.

One traverses the access to the terrace by crossing through an illuminated wall of alabaster bricks of vegetation.

An illuminated, planted facade evoking a giant chessboard, dominates the terrace.

The fundamental nature of this project is a harmonized integration of plants and architecture. Here, plants are treated as a surface covering, texture or skin. Their interplay with artificial materials is suggestive of a sort of hybridization or grafting. These reflect the design motifs inherent to the tradition of Louis Vuitton products.

Here, plants may be quickly and easily renewed and changed (bands of vegetation are simply velcroed onto exterior architectural elements). This design feature is suggestive of seventeenth century French gardens (Versailles) wherein plants and parcels could be changed and modified overnight.

Contemporary Logement Loft

Architects
Atelier Weygand Badani & Architectes,
Aude Borromée Architecte

Designer
Atelier Weygand Badani &
Architectes

Location
Paris, France

Photography
Laurent Gueneau

In Paris, the designers imagined a project made out of verticality and transparency while respecting urbanistic rules and integration in this quiet country side like place.

An internal organization where levels down (underground with light & ventilation; street level and level one) are made to work and levels higher (level two and three) are for living and sleeping. The low levels are more in contact with the street whereas the levels up are more related to the rear and connected to small terraces that can be completely opened. The last level (bedroom and bathroom) is even accessed by an exterior stair as if we were not in Paris anymore... In this last level we can imagine bathing almost outside!

The use of the colors to make space bigger, create different atmospheres according to the levels. Low levels follow the shades of the facade (burgundy, red, purple) and high levels are more in the blue and green colors.

The whole story of this project is to be understood through those five levels; their spatial, functional and aesthetic relationships and the sequence of atmospheres. Architecture and interior design are completely linked including those stairs that may be used to seat, the lifelines on which you can lean while talking and also with the customized drawings of the kitchen and bathroom work surface made of folded steel.

Dutch Energy Company Eneco's New Rotterdam Headquarters

Design Agency
Ambius(Plants interior)
Copijn(Green planting facade)

Interior Architect
Hofman Dujardin Architects in
collaboration with Fokkema & Partners

Architect Building
Dam & Partners Architecten

Client
Eneco

Location
Marten Meesweg Rotterdam,
Holland

Area
25, 000 m²

Photography
Matthijs van Roon

The creative Amsterdam firm Hofman Dujardin Architects, in collaboration with Fokkema & Partners, has played a leading role in helping sustainable energy company Eneco to practise what it preaches. They have designed the interiors for Eneco's headquarters building in Rotterdam, which has undergone a revolution to create the perfect working environment, complete with solar power, natural light and oxygen from internal vegetation, echoing Eneco's vision of sustainability. Eneco's new building is also the perfect example of how clever and efficient office design can offer employees the possibility to work flexibly in a dynamic, open, sustainable and healthy environment.

On top of everything else, there's more oxygen to breathe to keep employees healthy and alert, courtesy of the fact that the green plant walls on the outside actually make their way inside at the third floor, bringing the natural world into the built world.

Park Royal on Pickering

Design Agency	Architect	Location	Area
Tierra Design (S) Pte Ltd.	WOHA	Singapore	6,960 m²

Located within the Central Business District adjacent to Singapore's first privately owned garden — Hong Lim Park, Park Royal on Pickering is a demonstration of how greenery can be conserved even in a dense urban fabric not only catering to the users of the building but to the entire neighborhood.

The visitor's experience begins at the street level, where tropical greenery complemented by architectural elements blur the lines between where the neighborhood ends and the hotel begins. Strategic landscape veils any hard edges, and extends the greenery upwards as well as into the lobby and interior public spaces of the hotel.

A visually striking contoured podium is sculpted to create lofty outdoor plazas, walkways & gardens which flow seamlessly into dramatic interior spaces.

The crisp and streamlined tower blocks harmonize with surrounding high-rise office buildings. The lofty sky gardens which bring lush greenery to the rooms and internal spaces; corridors, lobbies and common areas with landscaping, stepping stones and water features create an alluring resort feeling with natural light and fresh air. The lush greenery is not only visually attractive but also offers environmental relief to its urban surroundings.

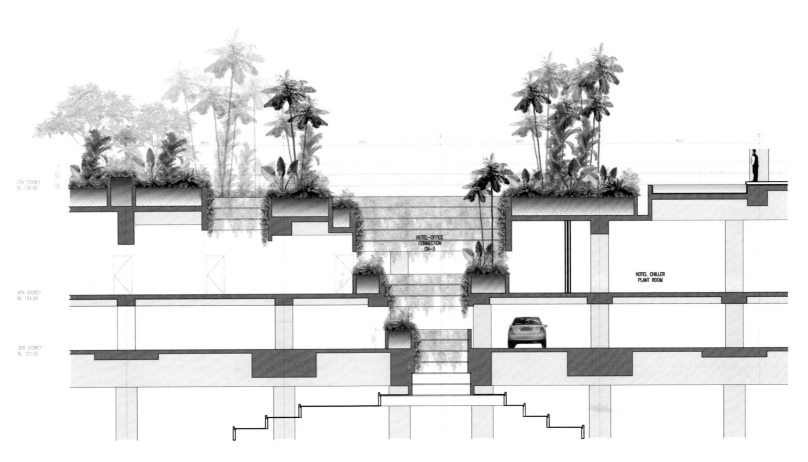

5TH STOREY
RL 130.00

HOTEL-OFFICE
CONNECTION
CN-3

HOTEL CHILLER
PLANT ROOM

4TH STOREY
RL 124.00

3RD STOREY
RL 121.00

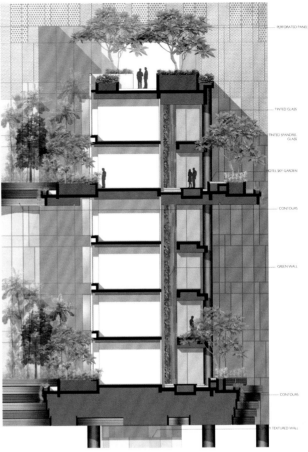

PERFORATED PANELS

TINTED GLASS

TINTED SPANDREL GLASS

HOTEL SKY GARDEN

CONTOURS

GREEN WALL

CONTOURS

TEXTURED WALL

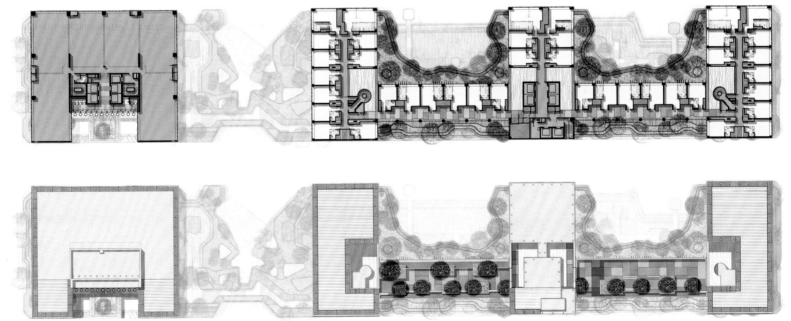

SmogShoppe

Design Agency
Woolly Pocket

Designer
Marvimon Productions

Location
Los Angeles, US

Photography
Suthi Picotte

SmogShoppe is a multi-use event space that was once a 1980's Smog Check station. Now powered 100% by solar energy, the LEED platinum event space hosts weddings, parties, films and PR events in a 604 m² (6,500 square feet) courtyard and pavillion. The courtyard is lined with lush succulent living walls that create a green backdrop for events; the outside of the SmogShoppe is wrapped in green walls that are visible from the street.

The SmogShoppe is located on a very busy, loud street. The primary design challenges were to dampen the sound from noisy street and the live reflective sound in the courtyard and to bring in more landscape. The pockets and plants, both on the outside walls of the complex and the interior courtyard served a powerful sound buffer, allowing the SmogShoppe to be a relatively quiet oasis in the city.

The green walls have served as an iconic backdrop to over 100 weddings and countless events. The large area given over to green walls on the property, allows the lot to have a 60% plant coverage. This represents a very high plant coverage for a commercial property.

Triptych Apartments

Vertical Garden Constructor	Architects	Location	Area
Fytogreen	Nettletontribe	Melbourne	206 m²

External facade from level 2 to level 6, over the southeast entrance, located in Melbourne's Southbank. Using a range of ground covers that are robust and tolerant to a range of weather conditions of around 20 species. Fytogreen's focus on Ecological Sustainable vertical gardens, ensure that the vertical garden species selected and located specifically for survival for the natural life of the plants species used. A botanist, who was invited to designed the array, has a swirling theme with the plants. Many flowering species are also used and an ever changing vista is seen as the garden ages. 300mm gaps provide airflow through 5 levels of car park behind.

Green Roofing Tile Cabin

Design Agency
Roel de Boer

The Green Roofing Tile Cabin is a project that ultimately shows how Roel de Boer aims to make the city greener on the one hand and stimulate the use of typical urban facilities, provoking social interaction on the other hand. It is a design in which concepts of different previous projects come together.

Since the city facilitates in practically everything we need in daily life, urban residences can be brought back to the essence. The Green Roofing Tile Cabin provides a place to sleep, the rest of the functions are spread out across the city where the wealth of facilities such as restaurants, coffee houses, cinemas, saunas, libraries, etcetera, will make other functions of the house unnecessary. Moreover, sharing urban facilities with fellow townspeople creates a strong social structure in urban life. Additionally, in this way the residence requires less space.

Cities have a large impact on biodiversity. By mainly using dense materials such as bricks and concrete, plants and animals are hindered in trying to settle, relocate or reproduce. In a joint search for a liveable and pleasant city we disregard the advantages of an ecosystem as a natural resource. Green in the city is generally enjoyed and seen as an added value in the street landscape.

To many people, plants and animals are an important source of inspiration. Moreover, the presence of nature makes us aware of concepts such as growth and time.

OLD HOLLAND

NEW DUTCH

Unique Lounge

Design Agency
mlapresse

Designer
Patrick Nadeau

Client
spoga+gafa 2012

Location
Cologne, Germany

Photography
Hervé Ternisien

Unique lounge was created for the SPOGA-Garden Fair in Cologne, Germany, which is the world's leading trade fair for the leisure and garden sector. It was the space in the fair that offered different services from meeting points to a welcome desk, from conference rooms to waiting and rest areas. Both urban and vegetal, these forms bring out a type of half-garden and half-architecture. Plants are integrated into all the different elements from the floors, to the walls and ceilings. The singular atmosphere of the place is defined by the playful interactions of small white flowers and the delicate materials used in the structure, which are made from perforated paper with backlit floral patterns.

Design Agency
Jardins de Babylone

Location
Paris, France

Area
30 m²

The basic idea of this project was to create a plant design in a narrow space and confined by high-rises buildings. The classic green wall was too big here where the idea of creating a framework to ease air space. The idea was to realize a plant abacus inspired Chinese abacus to count them.

The balls are here represented by movable sections of bamboo could create over the season and his desire for new plant

The Vegetal Abacus

design. The atmosphere of the space is lightweight, less opaque. Adding a mirror will enhance the depth to enlarge the space of the terrace.

3-meter bamboo cane was cut in sections of 30 cm and sealed for receiving plants. Top plate was made of a tube of 145 mm diameter cut at 45° for hanging bamboo. Each comprises a section of bamboo dropwise watering and evacuation.

Ideal Hotel

Design Agency	Location	Area
Jardins de Babylone	Paris, France	9 m²

What's better than green in the morning at breakfast for a good start from? This vertical garden in the breakfast room of the Ideal Hotel provides tranquility and pleasure thanks to this choice of vaporous plants.

An automatic filling system is located in the private kitchens of the hotel to ensure watering plant.

Green Symphony et Public au Taipei Concert Hall

Designer
Patrick Blanc

The living wall indoor is a great landscape under the soft light, providing fresh oxygen.

Sultan Ibrahim

Design Agency
Green Studios, Gatserelia Design Firm

Area
96 m²

Scope
Green Wall Main Consultant & Contractor

Client
Ramy Holding s.a.l

Location
Beirut, Lebanon

Photography
Green Studios

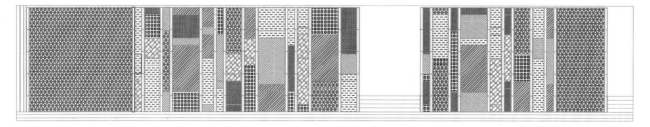

Linearity was the main theme for this green wall, having cor-ten sheets directing the rhythm vertically, interrupted horizontally by different types of plants. The main challenge for the Sultan Ibrahim green wall was its close proximity to the sea, with high levels of salinity affecting the plant palette as well as the need for yearlong monitoring of plant health.

Sweet Tea

Design Agency
Green Studios

Area
110 m²

Scope
Main Consultant & Contractor

Client
SOLIDERE, Moatti & Riviere
Architecture

Location
Beirut, Lebanon

Photography
Green Studios

Sweet Tea is the first one amongst these projects that includes a green wall installation; the restaurant's concept is an open sky terrace which 4 walls are treated in green wall.

The interesting part of the design is the reverse promenade, where the visitor, who normally transits from an outdoor garden to an indoor space is actually doing the reverse process; as you walk within the souks, you exit the urban to this tea shop where the walls are green and the sky is wide open and your senses automatically enter into a different relaxed mood, the sound of water adds on to the Zen character of the space and at night, the whole space is dimly lit on purpose that the visitor could somehow disconnect from the surrounding urban jungle.

The main challenges for the green wall were that it had both an indoor part with low light, and an exposed outdoor one. There was also a tent that covered the area compromising the amount of light that the green wall gets during the day , which puts the whole installation under constant stress.

Amazonia at the Heart of Restaurant

Design Agency
Jardins de Babylone

Location
Paris, France

Area
12 m²

The idea was to make this restaurant a corner of nature through the plant wall overlooking a jungle atmosphere with its abundant vegetation.

Located near the bar and kitchen, this 12 m² plant wall enjoys a beautiful canopy, and grow as nature intended.

Corsairfly

Design Agency
Jardins de Babylone

Location
Airport VIP Lounge, Orly

Area
20 m²

Installed in a VIP lounge in the Orly airport, this screen of plant allows creating a separation between the relaxation part and the cooks part. This openwork design brings the transparency and the lightness to the place.

Montreuil Showroom

Design Agency
Jardins de Babylone

Location
Paris, France

Area
13 m²

First showroom designed by Jardins de Babylone near Paris includes a tall plant wall. This vertical garden consists of a dry river pebbles dishes, giving the impression of a garden.

Located on a groundfloor and first floor, this 6.5m high green wall gives splendor to this place.

NS House

Design Agency
GALEAZZO DESIGN

Area
600 m²

Located in the city of São Paulo, this 600 m² house was designed to a family with the aim of being a place of social meeting among a collection of art and design. For coating it was chosen natural and sustainable materials like demolition wood for the floors and raw marble.

The social area was divided into sectors: living, cellar, dining room, gourmet kitchen and balcony. For decoration, vintage furniture mixed with Italian, French and Scandinavian design furniture. In all rooms there are Tibetans rugs made of wool and silk. At the entrance of the house a mirror receives the visitors in style.

The house was conceived with big windows and doors that allows daylight to be the big supporting element of the spaces. Despite the sectored ambient, all the house are integrated through spacious passages allowing the guests to enjoy the spaces with privacy but integrated to the house. The gourmet kitchen is the big venue where all spaces are joined together and it becomes the main attraction on the party nights.

In the big yard there's a pool for the summer days that magnifies the effect of oasis in an urban setting.

Vertical Garden in Replay Store, Barcelona

Design
Studio 10 Bianchi & Baccioni
Architects

Vertical Garden Consultant
Michael Hellgren

Location
Barcelona

Selling Area
815 m²

Green Area
111 m² + 30 m² court

Photography
Michael Hellgren et al.

Replay's store on Passeig de Gràcia in Barcelona hosts a vertical garden of just above 100 m². In the storefront location, the two storey wall is set in a dramatic and playful environment designed by Studio 10, with waterfalls, sculptures and contrasting materials.

As a great place to study nature's own vertical gardens, the waterfall was a natural starting point for the plant design. Looking closer to the environment around a waterfall, growing conditions change with linear patterns of fissures and cracks in the underlying exposed rock, or the rapidly decreasing moisture already small steps away from the immediate vicinity of the falling water. In such a manner, like the erratic and geometric cracking of an eroding rock, groups and strings of plants were laid out in an organic pattern.

The generous surface allows for many kinds of plants. Larger groups of begonias, different ferns, small (but long) aroids like the common

Philodendron scandens or Scindapsus pictus, set the background for more dramatic effects of cascading fronds of Nephrolepis exaltata and Polypodium subauriculatum or larger aroids like Philodendron giganteum and Philodendron erubescens.

The store also has a outdoor vertical garden, located in a patio in the back of the store. Partially shadowed by surrounding buildings, the southwest facing wall has the upper area well exposed to the hot mediterranean sun, whereas the lower part is mostly in shadow. This difference in sun exposure gave way for more typical mediterranean plants in the top — such as Lavandula, Rosmarinus and Artemisia — and more shadow preferring plants like Chlorophytum and Fatsia in the lower area. In between there are a few plants that will gain some more size, the idea being to create a strong and wild growing surface, contrasting the metal grid from which it extends.

Vertical Garden in Replay Store, Milan

Architect
Studio 10 Bianchi & Baccioni Architects

Vertical Garden Consultant
Arte Srl

Location
Milan, Italy

Selling Area
655 m²

Green Area
213 m²

Photography
Pietro Savorelli et al.

The new Replay store in Milan is the first flagship store to be completed using the concept that was first tested at the Replay store in Piazza Duomo, Florence. The principle inspirations are the same, but the store's skin has been adapted to the context, allowing it to sing.

A waterfall flowing along the entire length of the store plunges customers into an immersive experience, cut through 11 meters high monumental green walls where merchandise is regarded as part of the iconography connecting man to the elements. Nature has reclaimed man-made space with an impetuosity and a softness that is achieved in harmony with the spaces it

inhabits. These visual and tactile elements are the starting point from which to build, or rather rebuild, the relationship between man and the natural world allowing one to experience wonder and amazement across the senses. To access the main retail space, you have to cross the garden along a suspended walkway.

At the rear of the store is a steel wall that displays the shoes made by the brand. The theme of the wall is a recurring one: green wall, water wall, walls of wood and of steel. The wall in steel at the Corsia de 'Servi entrance to the store appears to crumble as if it were made in lumps of stone, a matrix that changes face constantly and is never the same.

Downtown Hotel

Design Agency
Cherem Arquitectos and Cherem
Serrano

Architects
Abraham Cherem, Javier Serrano
and Antonio Aguilar

Location
Mexico

Photography
Jaime Navarro

Located near "El Zocalo", right in the heart of the old city where the Aztecs first settled and afterwards the Spaniards built churches and palaces using the existing stones that were part of the Aztec pyramids.

"Downtown" is settled on a magnificent palace, witness of the 17th century architecture. Known as the "Palacio de los Condes de Miravalle", the red volcanic rock walls, the multiple doors, window quarry frames and the handmade cement tiles, along with the glorious patios and a spectacular stone-forge staircase provide the building the unique flavor of the Mexican vice regal style. The intervention preserved the original facades and the main walls, and although the designers took advantage of the general distribution of the space, a new order with a contemporary look was proposed, attributing a new identity and character to the building.

QUE BO!
CHOCOLATERÍA MEXICANA EVOLUTIVA
de José Ramón Castillo

EL JAPONEZ CDA Restaurant

Design Agency
Cherem Arquitectos and Cherem
Serrano

Architects
Abraham Cherem and Javier
Serrano

Location
Mexico

Area
235 m²

Photography
Manuhg

Bringing nature into the interior design was of big importance of the client, the designers wanted to create different environments that would evoke emotions and diverse experiences in the restaurant. With the help of landscape designer, Guillermo Arredondo, the designers designed a green module wall of hanging plants pots and drip irrigation system. This system is of simple construction and convenient for interiors. Considering the location of the restaurant and climate of Mexico City, local plants were selected to easily withstand the environment and minimize the maintenance. The textures of the plants soften the rigidity of the other walls creating contrast and style.

EL JAPONEZ Restaurant

Design Agency
Cherem Arquitectos and Cherem Serrano

Area
290 m²

Architects
Abraham Cherem and Javier Serrano

Photography
Jaime Navarro & Pedro Hiriart

Location
Mexico

A large open space, full of light, with virtually no columns, covered in wood and plants: design concepts that become reality in this restaurant. Vegetation is incorporated in an original way, and not by using weak elements such as flowerpots.

The floor of the restaurant is covered by a plastic carpet that evokes the tatami of japanese architecture.

The scarcity of columns is evident: only one column is clearly present in terms of space, which creates the impression that this long stretch is supported by only one structural element. There are other seven elements that playfully pretend to be columns but never touch the ground: they emerge from the soffit and have a specific role: the creation of two different environments within the same atmosphere. The rest of the columns have been hidden so as to avoid interrupting the flow of light and space.

The presence of wood as a material is not limited to the foreseeable use of floorboards, but contributes to the game of shapes and textures through the use of 10x10cm stud sections, which cover the solid sections and the soffit.

Over the bar, the stud wall shows some cavities, which are illuminated, making it appear less heavy and revealing that something happens behind them. A staircase hidden behind the bar leads to the rest rooms, which features an opaque glass box contained in another wooden box. There, the environment is milder, and it playfully pretends to minimize the separation between the men's and women's rest rooms.

The idea is based on small pots, made out of plastic pipes (pvc) that place together provide a water irrigation system.

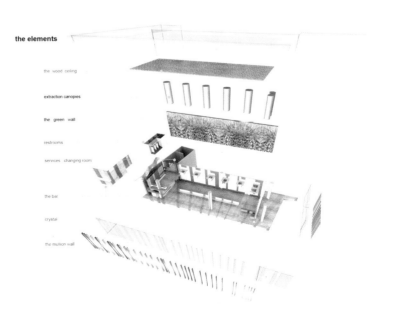

the elements

the wood ceiling

extraction canopies

the green wall

restrooms

services changing room

the bar

crystal

the mullion wall

Vertical Garden in Replay Store, Florence

Design
Studio 10 Bianchi & Baccioni
Architects

Vertical Garden Consultant
Michael Hellgren

Location
Florence

Selling Area
250 m²

Green Area
55 m²

Photography
Michael Hellgren et al.

The project at the new Replay concept store in Florence was completed in spring 2009, at the same time of the opening. The italian architectural firm Studio 10 based in Firenze has chosen Vertical Garden Design for the installation of this green artwork. The vertical garden was inscribed in the experimental environment of the new retail concept designed by the architectural firm for Replay and tested for the first time in Firenze. The green installation covers a 7m high L-shaped wall in the 3-storey boutique.

The garden is inspired by the undergrowth of a temperate forest, similar to what could be found in the lower parts of the hills not too far away from the city of Florence. Although as with any indoor garden, the plants themselves has to be mostly of tropical origin to do well in the indoor climate. The overall picture is a soft, yet dense, and fresh greenery, with some small-flowering plants like lanterns on top of the darker background. A picture that shall remind of the undergrowth in springtime, when it has had time to grow before the leaves of the canopy have fully developed and absorbed all incoming light.

There is a base of plants with medium sized leaves, like Aglaonema, Philodendron, Syngonium, Microsorum and a few other ferns as well. Within this framework, there are solitary species with stronger characters — like Begonia, Asparagus and Peperomia — some that are flowering, others with special colored or textured leaves. Usually, not too many solitary species are necessary to give the garden a distinct character, and actually a sparse use of these plants may better bring out their unique qualities.

As the wall is used as background for displaying the brands jeans products, hanging close to the wall, there is a limited space for using more voluminous plants. Thus, the size and growth habit were important criteria when choosing the plants. But still, as with any of these gardens, a certain pruning is necessary to keep a long-term viable garden.

Vertical Garden in Replay Store, Paris

Design
Studio 10 Bianchi & Baccioni
Architects

Vertical Garden Consultant
Arte Srl

Location
Paris, France

Selling Area
500 m²

Green Area
60 m²

This Replay store in Paris also focuses on the the design of vertical garden. As we known, in a traditional store, usually there is no connection with the natural environment and instead they often contrast sharply. There is no light or shadow, you don't perceive hot or cold and instead there is a constant ambient temperature and overexposed lighting. This environment principally lacks diversity. In the context of a store, the environmental conditioning is usually unsustainable. For this reason, vertical garden in Replay store borned.

Babylone Pendant

Design Agency
Greenworks AB Sweden

Projects
n.1 Intrum Justitia / n.2 Boffi Showroom
/ n.3 Police Station

Designer
Alexis Tricoire

Photography
n.1 Jason Strong

Babylone is a spherical plexiglass pendant with room for plants. The 50 cm sphere has five openings that allows stems and leaves to meander out of the globe.

The bottom of the globe can be covered with pumice that has a high water holding capacity and contains minerals and micro nutrients that feed the plants.

Moving Hedge
Room Divider

Design Agency
Greenworks AB Sweden

Designer
Alexis Tricoire

Projects
n.1 Intrum Justitia / n.2 Nordic Light
Hotel, Stockholm

Photography
n.1 Jason Strong / n.2 Per Ranung

Moving Hedge is a double sided plant wall on wheels with automatic irrigation system. The units are perfect as room dividers in office spaces or at creating recreational spots.

Moving Hedge is an intense green boost at any space that can benefit from air purification, sound absorption and overall aesthetic functions. Standard size 110×150 cm.

Plantwalls

Design Agency
Greenworks AB Sweden

Projects
Init, Restaurant Jonas, Central
Station Stockholm, Hemso, Ikano

Photography
Per Bäckström / Jernhusen (Station)

Wall surfaces that you want to cover with plants can be customized according to your preferences of plant design. In this case Greenworks takes care of the complete installation of the plant wall. The irrigation system is either integrated with the watering and plumbing system in the building or made as a closed system with a watering tank.

Just like green roofs, plant walls are perfect for introducing more greenery into urban areas. Not much space is required to turn a few square meters into gardens.

Nike Sportswear Store

Design Agency
Verde360°

Designer
Yael Ehrenberg Hellion

Architect
Sury Atié

Client
Iñaki Rozas/ Nike

Location
Condesa, Mexico

Area
280m²

Photography
Francis Vermonden and Yael
Ehrenberg Hellion

Located in the heart of one of the most trendy places in Mexico City, one can find the Nike Sportswear Store in the street of Amsterdam, La Condesa. The building that cradles this store is one of the old californian style houses that were built in the 19th century. The exterior of the house was renovated to conserve the old style, but the interior and the courtyard were done in a unique modern way.

The courtyard or former garden of the building had a multipurpose function. It was to be used as a recreational area and as a pass way for cars delivering material, so there was no space left for a normal horizontal garden and that is where the beauty of a green

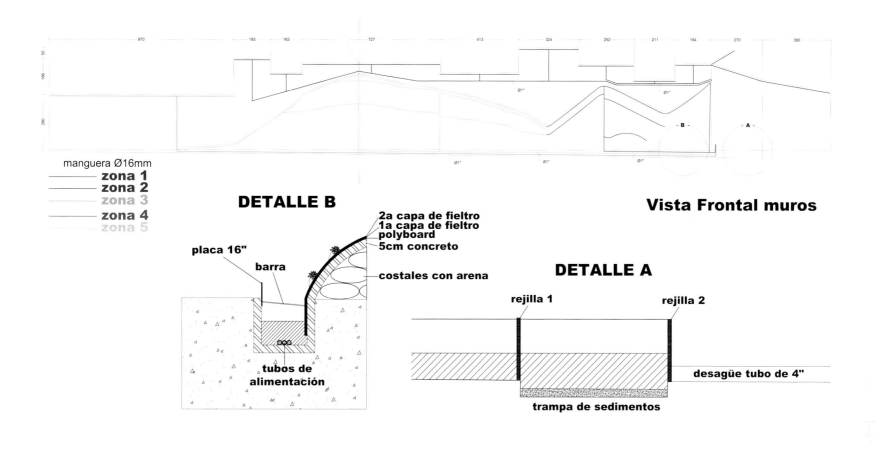

manguera Ø16mm
zona 1
zona 2
zona 3
zona 4
zona 5

DETALLE B

Vista Frontal muros

2a capa de fieltro
1a capa de fieltro
polyboard
5cm concreto

placa 16"

barra

costales con arena

DETALLE A

rejilla 1

rejilla 2

tubos de
alimentación

desagüe tubo de 4"

trampa de sedimentos

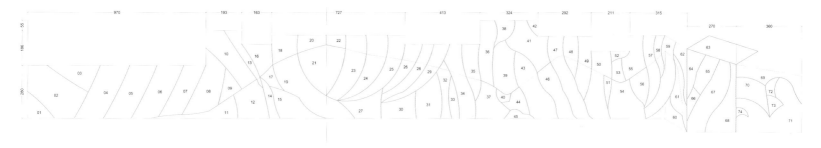

01.- Helecho chaquira
02.- Poligonia + Aralia Siboldi
03.- Vinca
04.- Trueno de venus
05.- Liriope verde
06.- Hemigraphis
07.- Duranta rastrera
08.- Muñecas + Iris caminante
09.- Pasto bambú
10.- Hiedra plateada

11.- Lagrimita
12.- Wedelia + Aralia Siboldi
13.- Trueno de Venus
14.- Lirio Amarillo
15.- Trueno de Venus
16.- Lirio Amarillo + Jazmin amarillo
17.- Mozaico rojo
18.- Poligonia + Jazmin amarillo
19.- Poligonia
20.- Iris Caminante

21.- Muñeca + Helecho silvestre
22.- Iris Caminante
23.- Duranta rastrera
24.- Iriope verde
25.- Hemigraphis
26.- Aretillo
27.- Violeta Tzamania + Cacomite
28.- Iris Caminante
29.- Vinaca Minor
30.- Helecho Cordita

31.- Pasto Bambú
32.- Lamium
33.- Helecho Boston + Acanto + Helecho Microsorum
34.- Wedelia
35.- Lagrimita
36.- Muñeca + Acanto
37.- Violeta Tazmanaia + Aralia Siboldi
38.- Mosaico Rojo
39.- Hiedra plateada
40.- Lirio amarillo

41.- Iris Caminante
42.- Lamium
43.- Helecho Boston + Acanto + Helecho microsorum
44.- Wedelia
45.- Lagrimita
46.- Muñeca + Acanto
47.- Hemigrafis
48.- Helecho Chaquira
49.- Liriope Verde
50.- Lagrimita + Acanto + Helecho silvestre

51.- Trueno de Venus
52.- Mozaico Rojo
53.- Pasto Bambú
54.- Violeta Tazmania + Acanto + Helecho Silvestre
55.- Violeta Tazmania + Acanto + Helecho Silvestre
56.- Muñeca + Acanto
57.- Duranta Rastrera
58.- Liriope Verde
59.- Liriope Verde
60.- Pasto Bambú

61.-Helecho Chaquira
62.- Vinca
63.- Vinca + Wedelia
64.- Iris Caminante
65.- Helecho Microsorum
66.- Helecho Boston "Blue Bell"
67.- Lagrimita + Acanto
68.- Liriope gigante + Liriope Verde
69.- Lirio Amarillo + Liriope gigante
70.- Lagrimita
71.- Lagrimita
72.- Mozaico coqueto
73.- Iris Caminante
74.- Helecho microsorum

vertical garden comes in. It was decided that the courtyard would have a ground cover of dark gravel and that the surrounding walls would be covered with a lush garden of plants, it would be a living wall that would contrast with the dark gravel of the ground.

The design of the living wall gives the illusion of a city, contoured with different heights as if it were buildings of different sizes, the lower part, designed with a slope creating an illusion of a mountain. The landscape designer chose around 38 different species of plants that could thrive in the climate

of Mexico City, 2, 600 m above sea level, with temperatures ranging from 12 to 28°C.

The living wall is fed by an automatic irrigation system with 5 irrigation zones. A section of the living wall is a room where the water tanks are placed and where the nutrients are poured in. The substrate of the plants is a 100% synthetic felt made of recycled plastic, so the plants have almost no soil and are placed in small pockets cut into the felt. Behind the felt is a plastic poly board made of recycled toothpaste tubes.

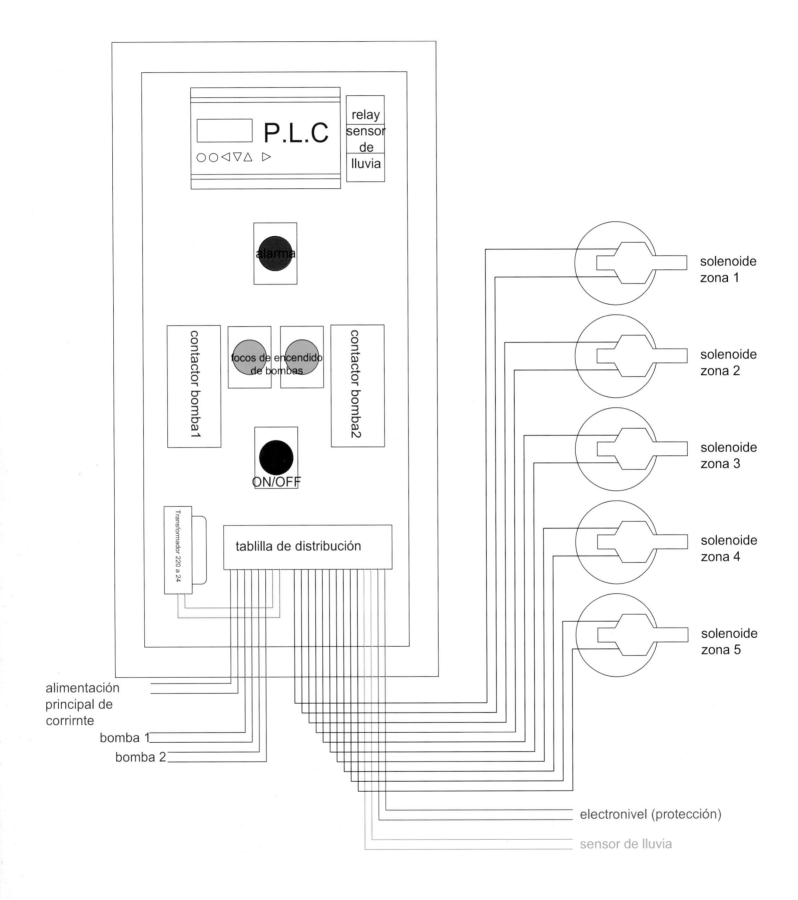

Tori Tori Restaurant

Design Agency
Verde360°

Designer
Yael Ehrenberg Hellion

Architect
Michel Rojkind

Client
Jack Zourasky

Location
Polanco, Mexico City

Area
254 m² of green wall

Photography
Francis Vermonden and Yael
Ehrenberg Hellion

Considered one of the best Japanese restaurants in Mexico City, Tori Tori is situated at the residential area in Polanco. It is an area that has seen changes in its zoning and houses have been transformed to offices or restaurants.

The Tori Tori restaurant was a house stripped completely of it's original facade and instead, a new facade consisting of two layers of steel plates gave way to mimic an organic pattern with openings filtering light, shadows and views that constantly invade the interior spaces.

Two living walls where created, a small interior one (24 m²) in the tea room and a large one (230 m²) in the exterior patio.

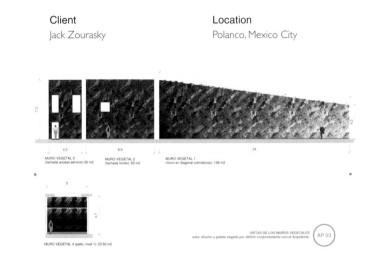

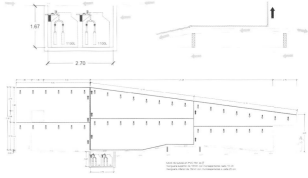

The landscape designer chose a very organic pattern, matching the organic movements of the steel plates of the facade. A rich and diverse number of plants where used to create a vertical garden with different tones of colours and textures. Some of the plants used for the horizontal garden where the same ones as the vertical garden to create a sense of continuity. The lush vertical garden has given a fresh live feeling to the enclosed space of the restaurants patio surrounded by tall buildings.

Café Banka

Designer	Architect	Location
Patrick Blanc	Mimolimit	Bratislava

Café Banka with a unique vertical garden has been opened in Bratislava. Green wall in the two-storey cafe J&T Café Banka is one of the most recent implementation of famous Patrick Blanc — botanist and the creator of Vertical Garden. Café, designed by the architectural studio Mimolimit, has been realized under the supervision of AED project. Vertical Garden consists of more than 2,600 plants of 66 various species.

New York Botanical Garden

Designer
Patrick Blanc

Location
New York, US

The New York Botanical Garden's 10th annual orchid show is designed by the famous vertical garden designer Patrick Blanc. The show was open from March 3 to April 22, 2012.

Freehills Offices

Vertical Garden Constructor
Fytogreen

Architect
BVN

Landscape Architect
360 Degrees

Location
Sydney, Australia

Area
60 m²

5 separate vertical gardens located on levels 26, 30, 33, 35, and 38 of an inner city corporate office in Sydney. Installation was done separately for each level and each with their own control system.

The planting plans for each level have an individual look to compliment the interior design of that level.

On level 26, 30, and 38 the vertical garden acts as

a backdrop to the staircase landing area. On level 33 the vertical garden is in a waiting space with TV viewing and city views.

On level 35 the garden is mounted on a "S" curved host wall creating a backdrop to the reception area.

Mahogany Room in Crown Casino

Vertical Garden Constructor
Fytogreen/John Patrick Landscape
Architect

Main Contractor
Baulderstone Hornibrook
Construction

Architects
Batessmart Architects

Client
Melbourne's Crown Casino

Location
Melbourne

Area
118 m^2

A series of 10 indoor vertical gardens made up of 5 walls in a row each facing each other. Above each host wall are skylights to assist with light levels.

These walls create a division between a VIP gaming area and quite reflective seating space. Built during the renovation of Crown casino's Mahogany Room. The design is based on Feng Shui principles to enhance the areas, aesthetic, while being Ecologically Sustainable for the species used.

Each "Fin" is 5m high and the plants used are all low light tolerant species that thrive in doors.

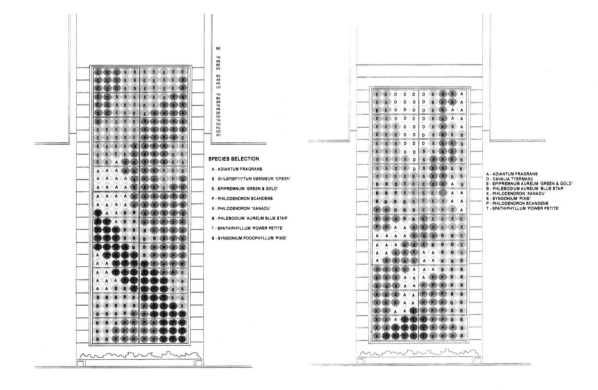

SPECIES SELECTION

A - ADIANTUM FRAGRANS

B - BILLBERGIA SOMBEUM 'GREEN'

E - EPIPREMNUM 'GREEN & GOLD'

P - PHILODENDRON SCANDENS

X - PHILODENDRON 'XANADU'

B - PHLEBODIUM 'AUREUM BLUE STAR'

T - SPATHIPHYLLUM 'POWER PETITE'

S - SYNGONIUM PODOPHYLLUM 'PIXIE'

A - ADIANTUM FRAGRANS

D - DAVALIA TYERMANII

E - EPIPREMNUM AUREUM 'GREEN & GOLD'

B - PHLEBODIUM AUREUM 'BLUE STAR'

X - PHILODENDRON 'XANADU'

S - SYNGONIUM 'PIXIE'

P - PHILODENDRON SCANDENS

T - SPATHIPHYLLUM 'POWER PETITE'

Indoor Vertical Garden Luxury Villa in Ibiza

Design Agency
Paisajismo Urbano

Location
Spain

This Indoor Vertical Garden, held in a private luxury villa in San Rafael, measuring thirty square meters. The species used for its realization are tropical undergrowth, belonging to ten species, for a total of one thousand plants.

The irrigation system, fully automated and remotely controlled, guarantees the stability and durability of this vertical indoor ecosystem, minimizing maintenance and providing the desired aesthetic solution that the property was looking for.

Indoor Vertical Garden Poncelet Cheese Bar in Madrid

Design Agency
Paisajismo Urbano

Location
Madrid, Spain

In June 2011, Paisajismo Urbano made the special Green wall for a famous restaurant in Madrid. An interesting work by the peculiarities of the restaurant, the owner wanted an artistic solution to renew the air and absorb strong smells of cheese.

The vertical garden is thirty-five square meters and contains a thousand tropical undergrowth plants from 15 different families, with the particularity of its exotic fragrances.

A success in terms of aesthetics and environmental solution, which distinguishes this restaurant and makes one of the most famous restaurants in Madrid to be known by its Green Wall.

Indoor Vertical Garden SPA
Hotel Castle Son Claret

Design Agency
Paisajismo Urbano

Location
Spain

This 43 m² Vertical Garden has been done in the SPA of the Hotel Castle Son Claret. It is a Vertical Ecosystem with 2, 000 plants from 15 different species, mainly tropical undergrowth. This created an organic design that fits perfectly in the location in which the heated pool SPA is located.

The complexity of this green wall lies in the high humidity and the lack of lighting. Species selection and design were instrumental in the setting and give the finishing look that the owners required, while maintaining the integrity of the Vertical Garden.

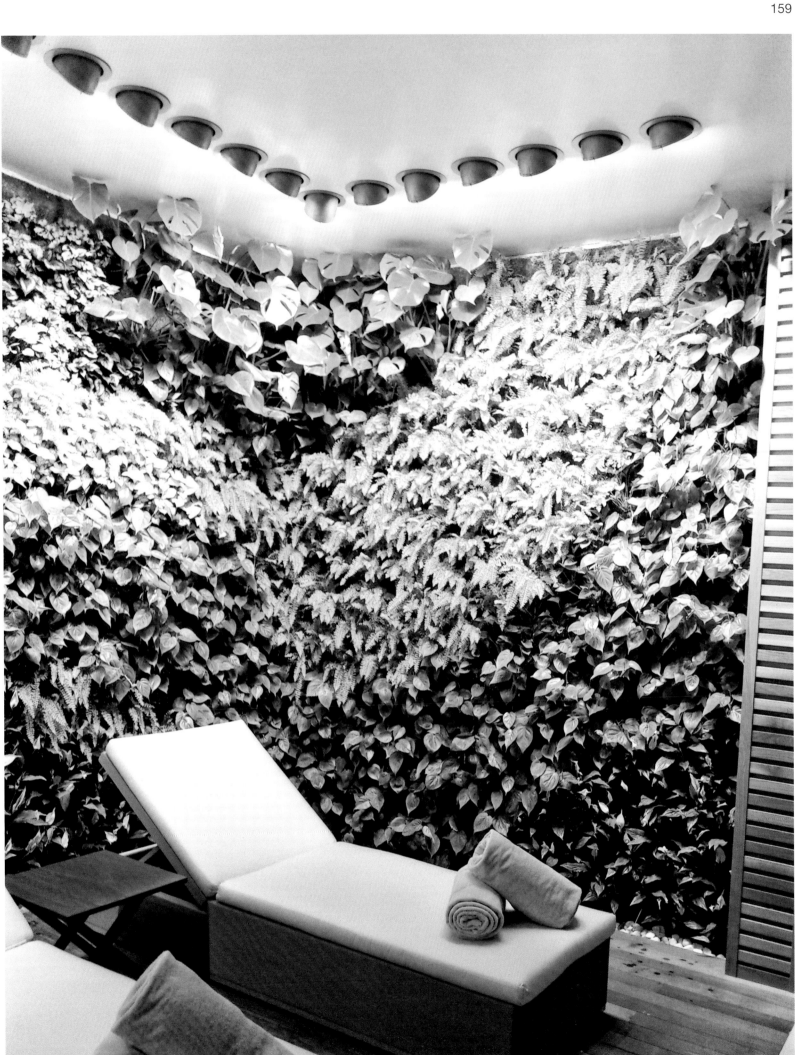

Mini-Farmery

Design Agency
The Farmery

The Farmery's retail area is a specialty gourmet grocery store, combined with a Café, and carries product categories common to these types of stores. However, The Farmery's unique design features such as the vertical hydroponic and gourmet mushroom production facility (within sight of the customers as they shop) on the upper level, the living river growing system and the opportunity for customers to pick their own product creates an unforgettable shopping experience that sets the Farmery apart from traditional grocery. The Farmery is a living building.

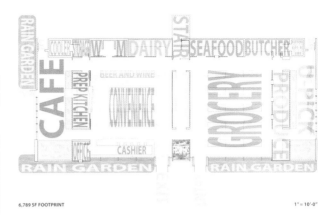

6,789 SF FOOTPRINT   1" = 10'-0"

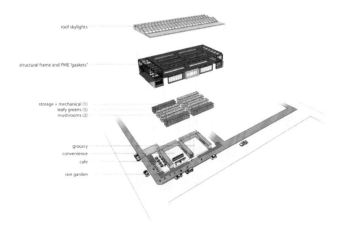

roof skylights

structural frame and PME "gaskets"

storage + mechanical (1)
leafy greens (5)
mushrooms (2)

grocery
convenience
cafe
rain garden

72 and Sunny

Design Agency
Woolly Pocket

Designer
Lean Arch

Location
Los Angeles, California

Photography
Woolly Pocket

The interior uses 270 Living Wall Planters in grey. The living wall is watered with a drip irrigation system.

Barbara Bestor Residence

Design Agency
Woolly Pocket

Client
Barbara Bestor

Photography
Woolly Pocket

Barbara Bestor is an award winning architect. Some of her astounding projects are in Los Angeles, like the Intelligentsia Coffee, and many homes like her current one showcased here.

We installed a huge edible garden outdoor right next to her pool. She has big sliding windows in her kitchen so whenever there's a breeze, it fills her home with scents of rosemary. Also, she can easily pick them from the window when she cooks with her family. Since Barbara Bestor favors mixing raw materials and vibrant colors, and creating a natural flow between indoors and outdoors, it was a no brainer to install a couple smaller indoor living walls. Living Wall Planters are great ways to greenify your space even if you don't have much space, so garden up and create a lush living painting!

Snog Productions

Design Agency
Woolly Pocket

Designer
Marvimon Productions

Location
Los Angeles, US

Photography
Dabito @ Woolly Pocket

At Call Me Faith Design Studio, interior designer Faith Blakeney likes to keep it green. She does this by using sustainable materials where she can, and plants to fill an environment with life and love. All of the desks are either custom made with reclaimed wood, or beautiful vintage pieces found at flea markets and the likes. The plants add a fresh, colorful design element, while oxygenating the air.

Her client, Deborah Burch, runs an ultra-hip, 360 degree Commercial Print, Video and Editorial Production Company called Song Productions. Her client list includes the likes of Bose, Sony,

Motorola, *GQ*, *Italian Vogue*, and UK Glamour.

In terms of the design, the key was to respect the industrial bones of the space while bringing the outdoors in; to create an environment which is as livable (and breathable) as it is functional. Deborah's team often spend long hours in the space, so it is essential that the loft serves as a workspace as well as a refuge.

Faith did not want to use precious floor space for plants, as this production studio at times holds as many as 15 employees and countless boxes full

of production material. Living Wall Planters provided them with the perfect way to bring nature into the space without taking up square footage!

Faith's vision for the space was 2-fold. The main office space (downstairs) brings nature inside, and with the large windows of the loft, almost gives the sense of being in a greenhouse. On the mezzanine they created the executive lounge. An intimate, inviting place where the CEO can meet with important clients. It is designed more like a living room, with a fantastic green view, thanks to their vertical garden.

Karoo

Design Agency
D&M

D&M is proud to present Karoo, a "green" concept for facades that adds an irresistible touch of greenery to any setting thanks to its simple indoor or outdoor modular system. Karoo is a Belgian product that was designed in partnership with the young product developer Jiri Vermeulen. The basic element is 40x40 cm and holds nine plants.

The fabric structure guarantees its attractive appearance.

A partnership with D&M resulted in a special kind of potting soil that is ideal for vertical installations. The modules are made of recycled materials and are available in dark grey and white. Karoo is quick and easy to install. Designed & Made in Belgium.

Capitaland, Six Battery Road, Rainforest Rhapsody

Designer
Patrick Blanc

Location
Singapore

Six Battery Road's vertical garden "Rainforest Rhapsody" is Dr Patrick Blanc's first project in Singapore and the largest indoor vertical garden in Singapore's Central Business District.

This vertical garden or also called living wall is designed by Patrick Blanc.

The principal benefits of the interior living wall, other than aesthetics, are the improvement of air quality and the reduction of interior temperatures, thus diminishing energy costs.

Capitol Clothing Shop

Designer
Patrick Blanc

Location
Charlotte NC, US

Juvia Restaurant

Designer
Patrick Blanc

Location
Miami, US

Juvia, the penthouse restaurant of 1111 Lincoln, is located blocks away from the Venetian Causeway on one side and South Beach on the other, a prime location in one of America's most celebrated design districts.

The patio is lined with a growing green wall designed by Patrick Blanc, a celebrated landscape architect who specializes in living walls like these.

8 Napier Road

Design Agency
Tierra Design (S) Pte Ltd.

Location
Singapore

Area
6, 774 m²

The design concept derives naturally from the physical nature of the site itself, sloping up from south to north from Napier Road to Nassim Hill Road. In a series of large, gently rising terraces, beginning from the grand entrance courtyard porte-cochere, Napier Residences orchestrates its experiences one wonderful landscaped level at a time. These grand terraces are gently and pleasantly accessible through wide steps and ramps. Tranquil reflecting ponds and gently overflowing waters create soothing sounds, culminating at a luxuriously tranquil 50 meter swimming pool at the site's highest point.

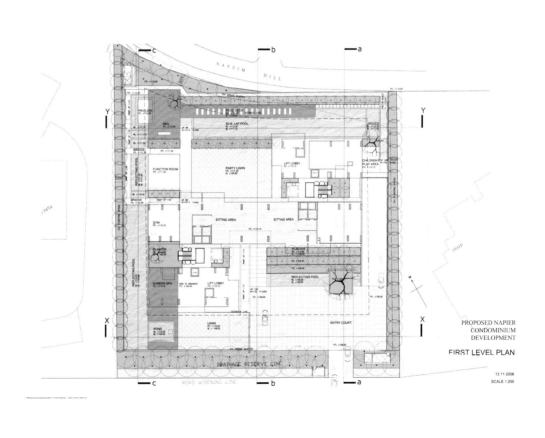

PROPOSED NAPIER
CONDOMINIUM
DEVELOPMENT

FIRST LEVEL PLAN

13.11.2006
SCALE 1:250

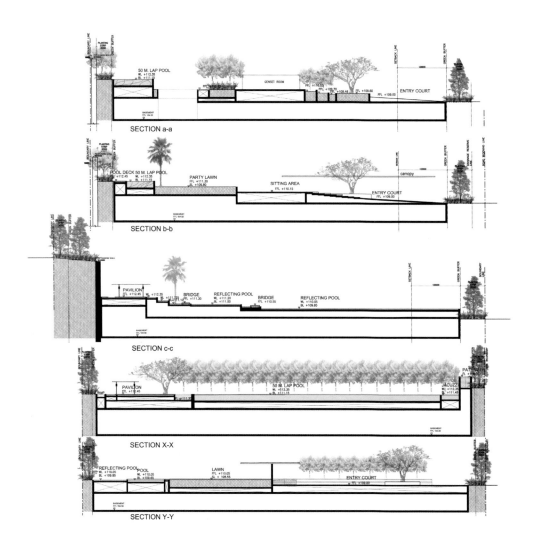

SECTION a-a

SECTION b-b

SECTION c-c

SECTION X-X

SECTION Y-Y

Upon arrival at the entrance, one is greeted by a quiet entrance court with a soft water feature in front. The entrance courtyard is a generous space anchored by an inviting canopy which seems to levitate over a verdant green "wall" bathed in natural light, below the large ETFE canopy. This green planting wall, together with its reflecting, overflowing pond, forms the main focus of the porte-cochere. Large sculptural flowering trees, with other surrounding lush green foliage, enhance the welcoming entrance courtyard experience. The

difference between the business of Napier Road and the serene court is immediately perceptible.

The entire landscape is tied together with tropical green, reminiscence of the botanical gardens nearby. Every level change is accentuated and lined with soft landscape, creating privacy and framing views.

8 Napier has evolved into a distinct elegant landscape with bold strokes of green and water.

158 Cecil Street

Design Agency	Location	Area
Tierra Design (S) Pte Ltd.	Singapore	1,075 m²

Although entirely indoors, the vestigial space of 158 Cecil, was really a left-over atrium created because of an allowed increase in area by the addition of new floors to the existing building. The challenge of converting the stark and barren areas into an elegant space allowed the team an opportunity to introduce vertical "Green Architecture" to this 7-storey interior atrium. A new facade (on Cecil Street) was created within the boundary line forming a recessed but external "Atrium" juxtaposed neatly with the existing receding floor plates within. To avoid need for sprinklers, fire fighting or smoke extraction system provisions, the "external" Atrium space needed to be naturally ventilated to meet local authorities' strict requirements.

The designers conceived the idea of a "Hanging Garden" within the existing architectural void with the design of a "layered glass" facade. The building's existing naturally vented architectural openings facing the street was in-filled with new "staggered-glass" panes by the architect to allow natural light and air to filter through while keeping out the occasional driving rain. The massive area of vertical planting visible from all interior floors to the building's 7-storey interior space, seeks to perform a visual function with the use of over 15 species and 50,000 plants.

This project has become a catalyst to encourage the concept of integrating architecture, interiors and landscape in creating many more holistically blended foci for Singapore as a 21st century liveable city, for all future cities.

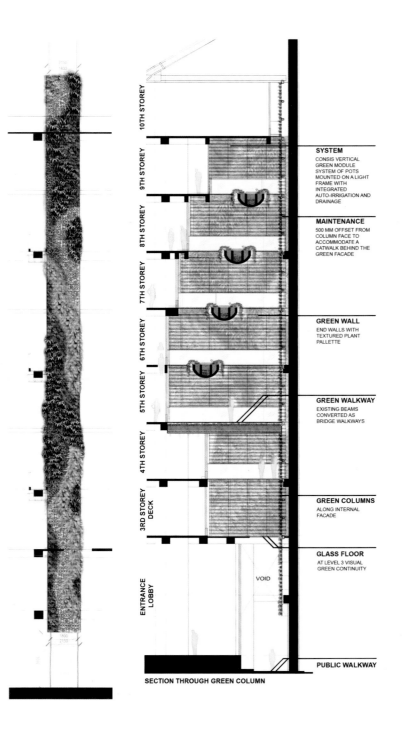

SYSTEM
CONSIS VERTICAL GREEN MODULE SYSTEM OF POTS MOUNTED ON A LIGHT FRAME WITH INTEGRATED AUTO-IRRIGATION AND DRAINAGE

MAINTENANCE
500 MM OFFSET FROM COLUMN FACE TO ACCOMMODATE A CATWALK BEHIND THE GREEN FACADE

GREEN WALL
END WALLS WITH TEXTURED PLANT PALLETTE

GREEN WALKWAY
EXISTING BEAMS CONVERTED AS BRIDGE WALKWAYS

GREEN COLUMNS
ALONG INTERNAL FACADE

GLASS FLOOR
AT LEVEL 3 VISUAL GREEN CONTINUITY

10TH STOREY
9TH STOREY
8TH STOREY
7TH STOREY
6TH STOREY
5TH STOREY
4TH STOREY
3RD STOREY DECK
ENTRANCE LOBBY

VOID

PUBLIC WALKWAY

SECTION THROUGH GREEN COLUMN

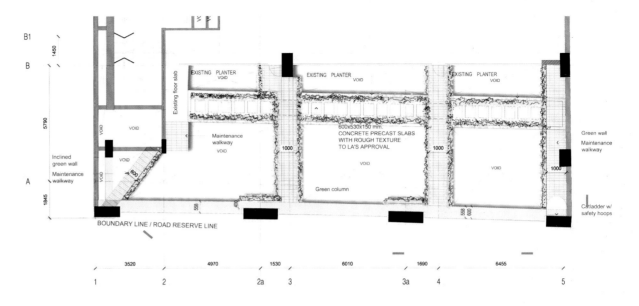

B1

B

A

1450

5790

1845

VOID

VOID

VOID

600

558

Existing floor slab

EXISTING   PLANTER
VOID

Maintenance
walkway

VOID

EXISTING   PLANTER
VOID

600x530x150 mm.
CONCRETE PRECAST SLABS
WITH ROUGH TEXTURE
TO LA'S APPROVAL

VOID

Green column

1000

558

600

EXISTING   PLANTER
VOID

VOID

1000

1000

Green wall

Maintenance
walkway

Catladder w/
safety hoops

Inclined
green wall

Maintenance
walkway

BOUNDARY LINE / ROAD RESERVE LINE

3520   4970   1530   6010   1690   6455

1   2   2a   3   3a   4   5

Miami Art Museum

Designer
Patrick Blanc

Location
Florida, America

In addition to elevated planters and trees rising through openings in a large open deck, 100 columns of planted vegetation created a museum atmosphere that can only exist in a tropical climate such as Miami.

Amazonica Floresta

Design Agency
Amazon Landscaping and Garden Design

In 2010 Amazon Landscaping and Garden Design were chosen from over 65 applicants to build their concept garden at Dublin's international Garden exhibition "Bloom" in the Pheonix Park.

The Inspiration for our Garden came from the Amazon Rainforest of South America. The Garden was influenced by the rare specimens of flora and fauna unique to the environment. We combined this ecological diversity with modern urban materials and contemporary design to create an exotic garden escape. Essentially the garden is a space to unwind in, surrounded by the beauty of natures abundance. Most gardens try to replicate this tranquility but often cannot duplicate the perfection of nature itself. This concept had a dual purpose, to display the natural superiority of the Amazon's architecture and to raise awareness of the destruction of the Greatest Living Garden on Earth.

The Living Wall was the centrepiece chosen to highlight this theme. The vertical planting of the wall was a representation of the Rainforest's Canopy and the Water blades simulated the many estuaries of the Rivers' meandering journey to the Sea. Individual planting was specially selected and pre-grown on panels for this purpose by expert horticulturists within Siempergreen, Holland.

The Garden itself was a huge success and definitely the People's favourite as it was the only large garden at the show to be auctioned and transported directly from the Park to the winning site in Naas, Co. Kildare.

San Diego Vertical Garden

Design Agency
Ricardo Marinho Paisagismos &
Amelia B. Lima & Associates, Inc.

Designer
Amelia B. Lima

Photography
Peter Carides

This was a joint project between the office of Ricardo Marinho Paisagismos and Amelia B. Lima & Associates, Inc. Ricardo had learned the technique from Patrick Blanc, the creator of this system, while working together to set up a show in Brazil.

In an effort to find a location for this vertical garden project, I focused on my own east facing side yard located in San Diego, California. The dinning room, and kitchen window overlooked into this area. The 1.8-meter (6-foot) tall concrete block wall was plain, and was set along the property line.

Suburban side yards are usually narrow and long, and very often limited by high block walls or fences. Vertical gardens seam to be the perfect landscape project to embellish these areas.

A water collection tank and a submersible pump was added to Ricardo's original design. My intent was to create a project that would be sustainable for the Mediterranean climate, where I live. A troth along the base of the wall channels the runoff water to a tank where a submersible pump re-circulates the water, several times a day. The system adds fresh water for only 3 minutes, every four days. Whenever fresh water is added, a soluble fertilizer solution is injected into the system.

The 24 m^2 (260 square feet) garden features a combination of soil-less epiphytes and lithophytes to create a Technicolor tapestry.

The vertical garden is supported by a galvanized steel structure set with concrete footing at a distance of one and a half foot away from the existing block wall. A layer of plywood and another

of PVC cover the entire structure. Two panels of felt were stretched over the PVC surface. Plants were inserted in small pockets cut into the top felt layer.

Gravel was used to finish the landscape and helped to conceal the water channel that runs along the entire length of the wall. Pre-fab concrete steps set in the gravel create a walkway and helps to carry the eyes along the wall.

The wall is now seven years old, and the plants seem to have evolved from the original design by spreading and reseeding throughout the wall.

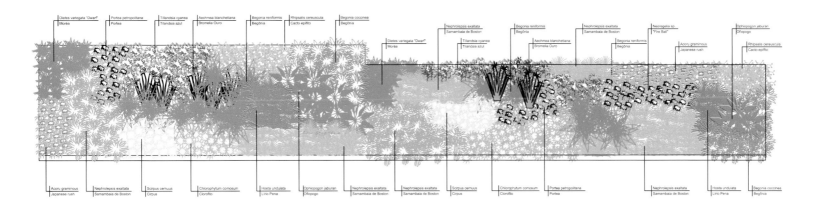

Dietes variegata "Dwarf"
Moréia

Portea petropolitana
Portea

Tillandsia cyanea
Tilandsia azul

Aechmea blanchetiana
Bromelia Ouro

Begonia reniformis
Begônia

Rhipsalis cereuscula
Cacto epífito

Begonia coccinea
Begônia

Dietes variegata "Dwarf"
Moréia

Nephrolepsis exaltata
Samambaia de Boston

Tilландsia cyanea
Tilandsia azul

Begonia reniformis
Begônia

Aechmea blanchetiana
Bromelia Ouro

Nephrolepsis exaltata
Samambaia de Boston

Begonia reniformis
Begônia

Neoregelia sp.
"Fire Ball"

Acoru gramineus
Japanese rush

Ophiopogon jaburan
Ofiopogo

Rhipsalis cereuscula
Cacto-epífito

Acoru gramineus
Japanese rush

Nephrolepsis exaltata
Samambaia de Boston

Scirpus cernuus
Cirpus

Chlorophytum comosum
Clorofito

Hosta undulata
Lírio Pena

Ophiopogon jaburan
Ofiopogo

Nephrolepsis exaltata
Samambaia de Boston

Nephrolepsis exaltata
Samambaia de Boston

Scirpus cernuus
Cirpus

Chlorophytum comosum
Clorofito

Portea petropolitana
Portea

Nephrolepsis exaltata
Samambaia de Boston

Hosta undulata
Lírio Pena

Begonia coccinea
Begônia

Painel para a parede na sombra

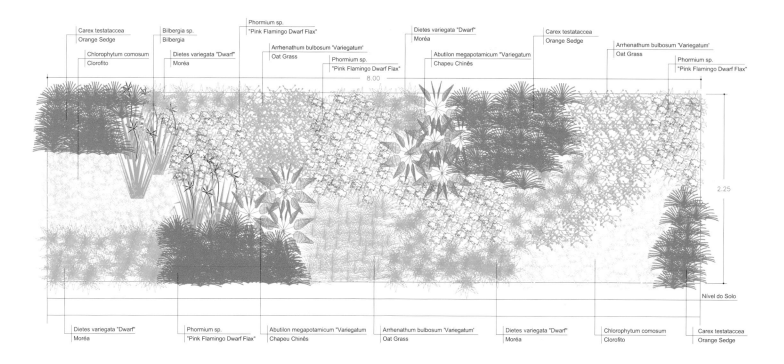

Carex testataccea
Orange Sedge

Chlorophytum comosum
Clorofito

Bilbergia sp.
Bilbergia

Dietes variegata "Dwarf"
Moréa

Phormium sp.
"Pink Flamingo Dwarf Flax"

Arrhenathum bulbosum 'Variegatum'
Oat Grass

Phormium sp.
"Pink Flamingo Dwarf Flax"

Dietes variegata "Dwarf"
Moréa

Abutilon megapotamicum "Variegatum
Chapeu Chinês

Carex testataccea
Orange Sedge

Arrhenathum bulbosum 'Variegatum'
Oat Grass

Phormium sp.
"Pink Flamingo Dwarf Flax"

8.00

2.25

Nível do Solo

Dietes variegata "Dwarf"
Moréa

Phormium sp.
"Pink Flamingo Dwarf Flax"

Abutilon megapotamicum "Variegatum
Chapeu Chinês

Arrhenathum bulbosum 'Variegatum'
Oat Grass

Dietes variegata "Dwarf"
Moréa

Chlorophytum comosum
Clorofito

Carex testataccea
Orange Sedge

Painel para a parede com sol

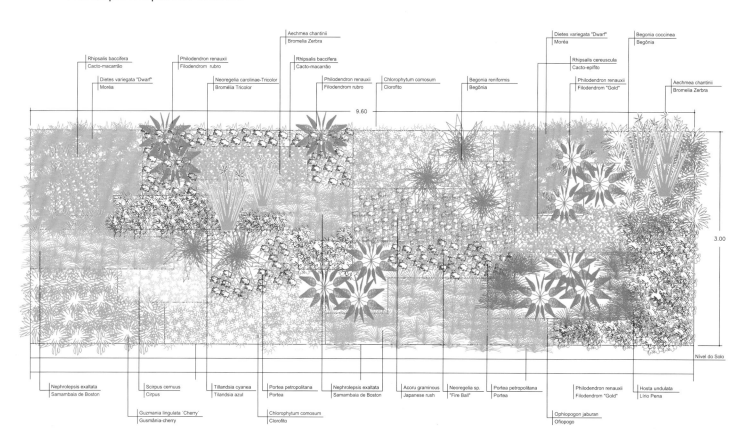

Rhipsalis baccifera
Cacto-macarrão

Dietes variegata "Dwarf"
Moréa

Philodendron renauxii
Filodendrom rubro

Neoregelia carolinae-Tricolor
Bromélia Tricolor

Aechmea chantinii
Bromelia Zerbra

Rhipsalis baccifera
Cacto-macarrão

Philodendron renauxii
Filodendrom rubro

Chlorophytum comosum
Clorofito

Begonia reniformis
Begônia

Dietes variegata "Dwarf"
Moréa

Rhipsalis cereuscula
Cacto-epifito

Philodendron renauxii
Filodendrom "Gold"

Begonia coccinea
Begônia

Aechmea chantinii
Bromelia Zerbra

9.60

3.00

Nível do Solo

Nephrolepsis exaltata
Samambaia de Boston

Guzmania lingulata ´Cherry´
Gusmânia-cherry

Scirpus cernuus
Cirpus

Tillandsia cyanea
Tilandsia azul

Chlorophytum comosum
Clorofito

Portea petropolitana
Portea

Nephrolepsis exaltata
Samambaia de Boston

Acoru graminous
Japanese rush

Neoregelia sp.
"Fire Ball"

Portea petropolitana
Portea

Philodendron renauxii
Filodendrom "Gold"

Ophiopogon jaburan
Ofiopogo

Hosta undulata
Lírio Pena

Home 06

Design Agency	Interior Build	Location	Area	Photography
i29 I interior architects	H2B interiors	Singel, Amsterdam	140 m²	i29 I interior architects

This residence at the Singel, Amsterdam (NL) exists from one open space where several functions have been put into freestanding objects. The kitchen and wardrobe are placed near the entrance and combined into one single volume.

The bath and bedroom is hided into a volume which is placed at back of the house. From the open living area you look alongside the volume towards the vertical garden and the entrance stairs to the roof terrace. The view on the green wall holds a promise in itself which will be redeemed once you enter the bed/bathroom. The small measurements of this combined bed and bathroom are in contrast with its spaciousness, while containing a private and personal feeling.

The panorama on the overgrown plantwall and the contrast with the minimalistic white bed/bathroom provides an intense experience. Integration of nature is an important aspect of traditional culture in Japan, the homeland of the client. The integrated in-house vertical garden is an example of this.

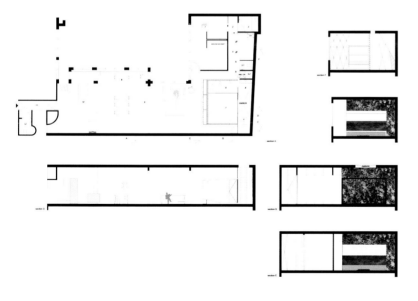

GLOBAL WORK et.

Design Agency
LIN inc.

Designer
Atsushi Suzuki

Location
Aeon Mall Kisogawa Kirio

Area
720 m²

Photography
Kozo Takayama

Fashion outlet for three brands — family brand "GLOBAL WORK", lady's brand "LEPSIM LOWRYS FARM" and interior items label "INMERCANTO" — boasting 700 m².

By placing "INMERCANTO" at the center of the shop, design of the interior allows customers to wander about to see all the different brands. Plants are installed over the facade and at the back of the counter as an icon of this shop, giving the space a feeling of open-air market.

Furstadtskaya Street Maternity Hospital

Design Agency
RaStenia

Client
Furstadtskaya Maternity Hospital

Location
St. Petersburg, Russia

Photography
RaStenia

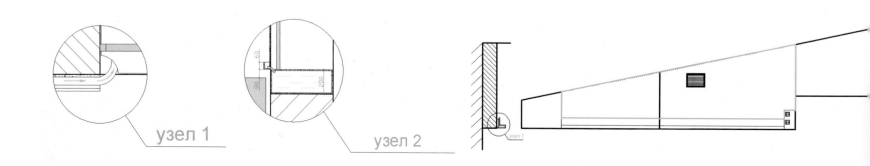

узел 1

узел 2

The Green Living Room of this maternity hospital has become even greener and a true living one with the exclusive greenery provided by vertical gardens. Designers had to solve the visual puzzle with the quadrangle hole in the room divider, and it was important to take into account all constructive features of this space. One of the water tanks is hidden into the white column.

Intensivnik

Design Agency
RaStenia

Client
Intensivnik Severo-Zapad

Location
St. Petersburg, Russia

Photography
RaStenia

The small room used for negotiations is virtually dominated by the large plantwall. The St. Petersburg progressive company Intensivnik was among our first customers in 2009. This construction was built later, when the company moved to the new office and needed lots of green elements there.

"Neskuchnyi Sad" Restaurant

Design Agency
RaStenia

Client
Neskuchnyi Sad

Location
Russia

Photography
Neskuchnyi Sad, RaStenia

Located in the central district of Rostov-on-Don, a large Russian city, this posh restaurant attracts customers by its unique atmosphere created with the help of a luxuriously cascading plantwall, some 24 square meters large.

NVIDIA

Design Agency
RaStenia

Client
NVIDIA

Location
Moscow

Photography
RaStenia

NVIDIA is a world leading IT-company, and it's no wonder one of the newest and smartest technologies in the floral market finds its place at NVIDIA Moscow office. The plantwall here serves more as a room divider and a nice accent, it is helpful in creating the overall homely atmosphere in this rather functional design.

The Living Wall with Plant and Stone

Design Agency
RaStenia

Location
Moscow

Photography
RaStenia

This is a private cottage for festivities and parties.
Cascading plants go well with the stone of walls.

Pushkin

Design Agency
Art-Studio, RaStenia

Client
Private Customer

Location
Str., St Petersburg, Russia

Photography
RaStenia

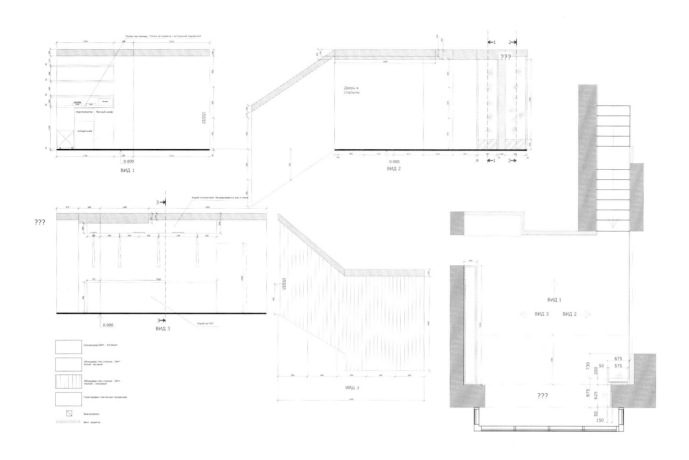

ВИД 1

ВИД 2

ВИД 3

ВИД 3

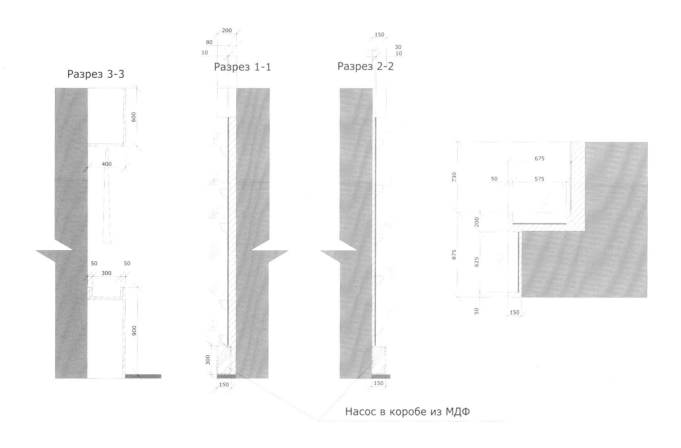

Разрез 3-3

Разрез 1-1

Разрез 2-2

Насос в коробе из МДФ

This suburban apartment is a home to three vertical garden pieces at once. Two of them are adding to the beauty of the relax zone, the third is placed in the hall, near the staircase. They are often being slightly restyled as the owner adores seasonal changes.

Vodokanal

Design Agency
Marina Dynai, RaStenia

Client
SUE «Vodokanal of St. Petersburg»

Location
St. Petersburg, Russia

Photography
RaStenia

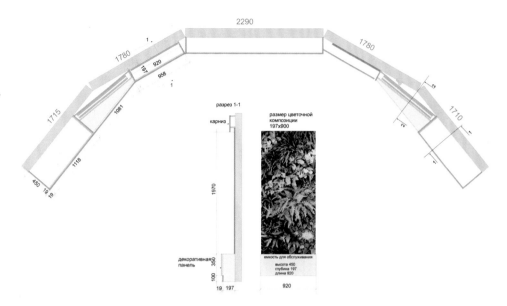

The composition of two plantwalls and a strip of potted plants was designed for the Childrens' Ecological Center working on the premises of the city's water treatment and supply company. This room serves educational purposes, kids gather here to watch documentaries on the living nature of the region. In design we tried to convey the visual image of North-West Russian forest zone.

Yanino

Design Agency
Viktoria Makarova, RaStenia

Client
Private customer

Location
St. Petersburg, Russia

Photography
RaStenia

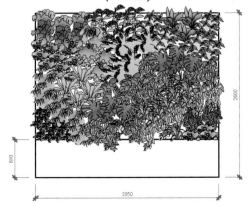

**схема рассадки растений в зимнем саду
(1-й этаж)**

2600

600

2950

Placed in a private customer's house in one of the suburbs, green walls decorate nearly all important home zones: sleeping room, bathroom, the study and, of course, the main hall on the first floor. The posh and bright greenery of the large plantwall is a decent substitute for a winter garden, very compact and manageable.

схема рассадки растений в спальне
(2-й этаж)

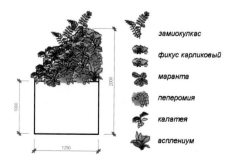

замиокулкас

фикус карликовый

маранта

пеперомия

калатея

асплениум

Rustic Canyon Residence

Design Agency
Airplantman

Designer
Josh Rosen

Location
Santa Monica, CA

Photography
Airplantman

When solar panels were added to the roof of this spectacular house designed by Ray Kappe, the client hoped to maintain their view while screening the new addition and creating a design that celebrated their passion for airplants. Airplantman transformed the rooftop space with a living tillandsia wall. Sixteen lightweight AirplantFrames are arranged on a trellis with a textured backdrop of Spanish moss tillandsia usenoides.

Tinga Restaurant

Design Agency
Airplantman

Designer
Josh Rosen

Photography
Bill Ryan Photography

Landscape architect Josh Rosen — also known as Airplantman — has developed a unique form of vertical garden devoted to soilless tillandsia. Ideal for airplant display and care, the AirplantFrame seamlessly displays airplants in custom designed frames that highlight tillandsia's airborne nature and amazing diversity of color and textures.

Tillandsia or airplants live suspended in air without need of soil or any growing medium. Inspired by this unique ability Airplantman creates transparent vertical gardens that function both wall mounted or as living screens, allowing air and light to pass through. The AirplantFrame has a modern minimalist aesthetic character highlighting the dramatic form of tillandsia, while also encouraging nurturing air circulation and easy watering to ensure plant health in a variety of environments.

The AirplantFrame modular system allows for a wide range of applications without technological or structural requirements challenge. Airplantman's installations are featured in private residences, commercial, office, and hospitality spaces; each memorable and engaging work of living art capturing the imagination and defying expectations. The beauty of Airplantman's design is its flexibility, simplicity, and creativity — rearrange the plants to create an interactive vertical garden that engages people, space, and light.

A note on Tillandsia — they are a genus of plant in the Bromeliaceae family. They evolved to inhabit environments without soil such as treetops or bare rock. Their leaves have the ability to directly absorb water and nutrients, with roots only being used to secure the plant. Tillandsia are epiphytes and not parasitic upon their hosts. The tillandsia genus is extremely diverse, with over 600 species known. The plants are found across the southern United States through Central and South America in a variety of ecosystems ranging from rainforests to deserts. This diversity of habitats has lead to an incredible range of colors, textures, and forms.

Vertical Garden Penthouse in Murcia

Design Agency
Paisajismo Urbano

Location
Murcia, Spain

The Vertical Garden in the city of Murcia is located in a private South facing penthouse. This Vertical Ecosystem consists of 70 square meters, have 2,000 plants of 30 native Mediterranean species adapted to the harsh weather conditions of the area.

The owners of this penthouse wanted to enjoy a green oasis in a sea of asphalt and bricks, to rest from the stress of their daily lives.

Moss Your City

Design Agency
PUSHAK Architects

Moss Your City is a first price in an invited competition for the Architecture Foundation and London Festival of Architecture. The brief was to explore the relationship between modern architecture and Norwegian nature, and at the same time responded to local conditions in London.

The designers proposed to use the gallery as a showroom for existing green forces in the area; it includes Guerilla Gardeners, Bankside Urban Forest and various other green initiatives. Designers wanted to encourage everybody to be gardeners in their own city. On the web the designers found a recipe for moss-graffiti. With the intense color and fragrance of the moss, visitors could get the feeling that nature had arrived in the city.

Rommen

Design Agency
PUSHAK Architects

Client
Municipality of Oslo

Location
Oslo, Norway

The overall scheme is based on an exsisting masterplan that gave two rows of housing surrounding a shared green space. Within these frames the houses are angled in plan and section to optimize use of solar energy. The roofs have solar collectors and the facades have large windows towards the south. Greenery is used for solar shading in summer. The development will have passive house standard, with minimized use of energy.

Nøtteskogen

Nøtteskogen danner en privatiserende buffer langsmed hovestien i felleshagen. I nøtteskogen kan man søke stillhet på små intime plasser som er av fra lekeplasser/ssene, eller man kan sitte med ryggen mot skogen og nyte solen. Skogen består av vanlige hasselntrer, trollhassel/vrihassel og valnøttrer.

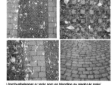

Utomhusbelegget er tenkt som en blanding av gjenbrukt stein/ markstegl og grus.

Frukthagen

Frukthagen ligger innenfor og utenfor gjerdet til barnehagen. Frukttrærne kan være epletrær, moreltrær, kirsebær, grspære og plommetrær.

Klatreplanter

Klatreplanter som skal vokse på netting/ssedlene er villvin, clematis, rdikartbusk og humle. Humlen vokser raskt, og kan fylle hele veggen første sommeren. Den vil kunne fungere som en semmeplante som skaper bedre forhold for de andre plantene. Bruk av ulike typer clematis vil gi planter som blomstrer til forskjellige tider av ssasongen, og som har forskjellige farger.

Hekker med spiselige frukt og bær

Hekkene som fungerer som buffere for de private hagene består av hyllebrbusker, tpsbusker, svartsurbærbusker, rogn og slbvedd.

Valg og plassering av vegetasjon er gjort i samarbeid med Lise Adelsten, hagedesigner og antkppsgartner.

ION Orchard and The Orchard Residences

Design Agency
Tierra Design (S) Pte Ltd.

Design Consultant (Overall Building Form and Facade)
Benoy Singapore

Architect
RSP Architects Planners & Engineers (Pte) Ltd.

Client
Orchard Turn Residential Development Pte. Ltd.

Location
Singapore

Area
18,652 m²

The integrated development of ION Orchard and The Orchard Residences is an award winning urban design that holistically transforms the central node at Orchard Road into a state-of-the-art commercial, shopping, entertainment and residential centre. This project was part of the city's initiative to stimulate existing activities, catalyse renewal and redevelopment in this premium commercial precinct.

The challenge of landscaping one of the busiest pedestrian malls in Singapore meant that the design had to blend convenience and functionality with beauty. Clean, open sidewalks and elegant steps and ramps invite visitors of all ages — mothers with prams, the elderly and physically challenged to experience the mall's glamour.

Lush greenery punctuated the walkways along Paterson Road and Orchard Boulevard. A verdant vertical wall, spanning 60m in length and 3m in height lines the building along Orchard Road. To enhance this vertical garden, shards of stainless steel troughs are used, adding a touch of randomness and punctuating the evening with a rhythm of lights.

The landscape design for the ninth-storey terrace garden of the super luxury The Orchard Residences neutralises the busy surrounding cityscape with a tranquil environment. Flowering trees scent the water and the air. Carefully designed water features and reflecting pools ensure that the sound of running water is heard throughout the terrace. Natural materials in the water features, the planting, ramps and the gazebos create a sense of warmth and intimacy with nature within the urban oasis.

Elevation along Orchard Boulevard

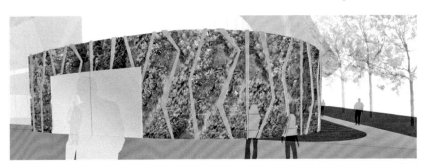

Perspective View along Paterson Road

Orchard Turn Mixed Development
Green Wall Elevation & Perspective

ORCHARD TURN MIXED DEVELOPMENT
1ST & 2ND STOREY - GREEN WALL
ORCHARD BOULEVARD

The Coast at Sentosa Cove

Design Agency
Tierra Design (S) Pte Ltd.

Location
Singapore

Area
25, 685 m²

With its tranquil location on the eastern coast of Sentosa Island, Sentosa Cove is Singapore's most exclusive marina residential community offering tropical resort living just minutes from the bustling city life on the mainland. As an integrated waterfront resort concept that blends residential, commercial and marine facilities, Sentosa Cove promises a lifestyle without equal not only in Singapore, but also across the region.

The landscape at The Coast at Sentosa Cove, epitomizes the experience of water-front living through its series of transitions. Coming from the city and stepping into a sanctum of tranquillity, one experiences living by the ocean. The sound of trickling water merged with the meditative surroundings make the environment pure and breath-taking.

Extending the waterfront lifestyle, the landscape consists of a large expanse of water consisting of lap pools, shallow pools, spa pools, leisure pools, reflecting pools and cascading pools all around. All first storey units enjoy exclusive direct access to shallow pools as an extension of their private enclosed spaces. These shallow pools serve as a buffer for the residents from the public areas beyond. Decks dotted around provide interactive spaces for pool side activities. This is the "Beach" side recreation area designed for the residents since there is no access to a natural beach.

Albizzia House

Design Agency	Architect	Interior Designer	Site Area	Building Area	Photography
Metropole Architects	Nigel Tarboton	Union 3 Clifton Smithers	4, 360 m²	1, 000 m²	Grant Pitcher

The designers were commissioned to design a contemporary family home on a one acre (4, 046.8 square meters) site, situated at the end of a spur, in Simbithi Eco-Estate. The client's brief called for a home with an overriding sense of simplicity but with a high degree of sophistication. All the living areas and bedroom suites face onto a panoramic vista, which includes a dense forest down-slope from the house.

The architectural style of the home is heavily influenced by the "Googie" architecture of the American architect John Lautner. The origin of the name "Googie" dates to 1949, when architect John Lautner designed the West Hollywood coffee shop, Googies, which had distinct architectural characteristics.

"Googie" was also characterized by design forms symbolic of motion, including upswept roofs, curvaceous geometric shapes, and the bold use of glass, steel and neon, the spirit of which is embodied in Albizzia House.

Nature Individuelle

Design Agency
mlapresse

Designer
Patrick Nadeau

Location
Philippe Chancel

Tables, planters, shelving and walls of vegetation reveal a singular vision of landscape and landscaped living space. These project is make in collaboration with the biologist Mathieu Jacobs, a specialist in the cultivation of groundless plants. A furniture and object series, the work proposes innovative concepts for the integration of vegetation in domestic habitat.

Containers and surfaces

Entitled "Individual Nature" the show presents two types of objects. The series entitled Planters and Groundwork (pot, rocaille or tontine in French) are containers. Revised and modified plant receptacles invoke the concept of the transformed, enlarged, redevised flower pot. The Relief and Horizon series are surfaces that extend into space like topographical reliefs overgrown with a carpet of ground cover. Nadeau's designs exploit two techniques. The first consists of enmeshing planted material in 3-dimensional textile. Thus contained, the nourishing substrate can be placed or inclined in different positions. Another technique called tubes and specimens employs the principle of Plug-and-Play: each plant is inserted into a cavity

created in the substrate (of earth, clay pebbles, or gravel layering). The ensemble of plant and substrate are conceived to be easily replaced with a change of season or of mind.

The objects as support

Invading the under-surface of shelving, a desk's edge, or climbing a screen wall, nature as proposed by Nadeau, is not to be circumscribed or contained by a common vision of flower pots or little gardens. His distinct conceptions dramatize nature: seeking to establish an intrinsic dialogue, they infer the possibility of organic extension; vegetation is lightly, delicately set forth by its architectural support. Quite simple in the formal sense, these "supports" characterize Nadeau's attentive aesthetics and careful designs: light undulations or subtle curves of noble materials (Corain®, Dacryl®, ceramic or leather...) where elegant natural compositions punctuate the surface. The true design always emerges from the living plant material: vegetation, set forth in an array of perspectives, flourishes in all of its inherent diversity.

KKCG

Design Agency
VRTIŠKA • ŽÁK / RAW ATELIER

Area
8,500 m²

Newly renovated office building in Prague was designed by Prague based studio VRTIŠKA • ŽÁK, together with a Brno studio based RAW ATELIER. The client is an international business company, focused on an environmental sustainability.

This project purely reflects natural approach and materials. The goal was to create dominant item of the building interiors is a 21m height vertical garden, where the plants are grown. The moisture system is computer controlled. Another eyecatcher, once you enter the main lobby is a white polygonal "interior facade" made out of laquered aluminium profiles. It gives to the lobby dynamic, yet calm feeling. All together combined with a laquered glass claddings, corian reception and a barrisol lightup ceiling.

In this ground floor, you can find an office restaurant with a foyer facade looking ceiling. Here the principle was placed in a horizontal position to make a floating effect of the ceiling and to cover the installations. The space is divided again with vertical green wall.

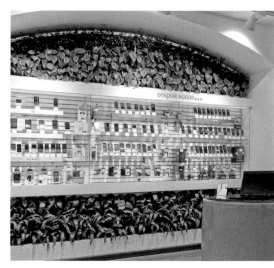

Design Agency
RaStenia

Client
MEGAFON Moscow

Location
Moscow

Photography
RaStenia

MEGAFON Retail Store

This fresh solution for a largest mobile operator's retail zone is a good illustration to the idea that plantwalls may be very versatile in form and outline. Plants have rapport with the corporate "grassy" style of MEGAFON.

Contributors

Airplantman

Airplants have a personality all their own. Thumbing their nose at convention, airplants live without soil, free in the air. Mild mannered Josh Rosen was captured by their powerful allure and Airplantman was Born.

On the go and with limited space, Airplantman needed a creative solution to display and care for his beloved airplant entourage. Not just any design would do; it must elevate airplant display to an art form, be simple to use and healthy for airplants. As a landscape architect, artist, and horticulturalist, Airplantman was up to the challenge. Built with an eye for fine design, craftsmanship, sustainability, and a genuine obsession for all things airplant, the Airplantman Designs product line was introduced to the world.

Amazon Landscaping and Garden Design

Amazon Landscaping and Garden Design provide Award winning Landscape Architecture and Garden Design from Dublin, Ireland.

After gaining experience with established Horticulturists, Designers and Contractors, Edward Cullen set up his own Landscaping and Garden Design business in 2005.

Currently studying with the Royal Horticultural Society Dublin, Edward's portfolio includes unique and inspiring projects from large scale rural developments to chic urban transformations around the capital ranging range from functional family gardens to private minimalist retreats.

One of Dublin's only members of both the Association of Landscape Contractors of Ireland and the Guild of MasterCraftsmen Amazon Landscaping has won a total of 5 national awards in 2013 and 2014.

Amelia B. Lima & Associate, Inc.

Amelia B. Lima & Associate, Inc. is a landscape design office located in San Diego California, that specializes in residential designs.

The gardens created by the office are well suitable for the local climate, and Amelia strives to create gardens with visual impact that complements the house's architecture, while offering a sense of place.

Amelia was born in Rio de Janeiro, Brazil, where she studied architecture. She holds a degree in horticulture from a College in Illinois. In the 32 years that she has lived and worked in the United States, Amelia has created gardens in Illinois, Ohio, Massachusetts, Texas and California.

ART arquitectos S.C.

ART arquitectos S.C. is dedicated to architecture and interior design. It has offices in U.S.A. and Mexico, and has won numerous awards.

Atelier Weygand Badani & Architectes

Atelier Weygand Badani & Architectes
6 bis, villa Santos Dumont / 75015 Paris / T 01.46.47.98.17 / F 01.47.03.98.90
E-mail : atelier@wbarchitectes.fr / Web : www.wbarchitectes.fr

Atelier Weygand Badani & Architectes is an architectural and design company in Paris established by Antoine Weygand in 1997. With over 17 years experience in the architectural field the company possesses vast and extended experience in a large variety of constructions, such as public libraries, multi-purpose halls, crematoriums, apartments, industrial and office buildings.

Our team is always seeking for innovative solutions and the harmony between the heritage of the existing environment and the new constructions. The guideline of our work is to follow a simple and consistent logic in a global scale and provide a richness of the details at the same time. In order to achieve the quality of the project a technical knowledge of the matters and the materials is essential.

Our commitment is to create buildings in which functionality, beauty and ecology combine. The devotion our company shows to architecture, the respect and the functional skills are our assets to create harmony between these values.

Bianchi and Baccioni Architects

STUDIO 10
BIANCHI E BACCIONI ARCHITETTI

Roberto Baccioni and Simona Bianchi, both born in 1970, work together since 2001. They have different features and skills coming from complementary training experiences. Simona Bianchi had an education focused on interior design and restoration. In the early years of her career, she worked in one of the most renown Florentine practices for the restoration of historical buildings. She took part in the restoration design of many Florentine palaces dating back to 15th and 16th centuries and designed houses for prestigious clients. Many of the historical buildings' restorations listed in the Currriculum of Studio 10 were carried out directly by Architect Simona Bianchi. Together with a great capacity of project development, she has excellent organizational and management skills that enable her to be the most appropriated person for the coordination of collaborators. Roberto Baccioni developed strong technical and construction skills thanks to a multifaceted training. These expertises make him able to turn the design into a process with a high rate of efficiency both for the technical and economic optimizations. The internal job in the office is always the result of a very strong collaboration among these different members and their skills: a constant supervision of the directors and the perfect synergy of the internal competencies, assure a high quality to every project.

The partnership between Roberto Baccioni and Simona Bianchi began by designing museum stands and the refurbishment of luxury houses between 2001 and 2004. From 2005 to 2007, together with a third partner, architects Bianchi and Baccioni focus their effort on a new design process integrating and coordinating technical and design aspects which places them on the cutting edge for their ability of control over projects with a high level of complexity. The considerable technical know — how is a solid background for the aestethic and emotional aspects of every project. The importance of design is strongly connected to managment and operative skills since there are no aesthetic solutions without a high technical profile. In 2007 architects Bianchi and Baccioni decided to establish a practice focused on design, They chose to locate it in a former artist workshop, studio n.10. From then on their engineering experience is a solid background for better focusing on emotional and aesthetic aspects of design. The poetic vision of the studio is to continue moving towards the use of natural materials in projects. This direction is supported by progressive research based on the notion of "natural living" and on mankind's desire to reconnect itself to space and to the resources that it has at its disposal.

Carlo Ratti

An architect and engineer by training, Carlo Ratti practices in Italy and teaches at the Massachusetts Institute of Technology, where he directs the Senseable City Lab. He graduated from the Politecnico di Torino and the École Nationale des Ponts et Chaussées in Paris, and later earned his MPhil and PhD at the University of Cambridge, UK.

Carlo holds several patents and has co-authored over 250 publications. As well as being a regular contributor to the architecture magazine Domus and the Italian newspaper Il Sole 24 Ore, he has written for the BBC, La Stampa, Scientific American and The New York Times. His work has been exhibited worldwide at venues such as the Venice Biennale, the Design Museum Barcelona, the Science Museum in London, GAFTA in San Francisco and the Museum of Modern Art in New York.

Carlo has been featured in Esquire Magazine's "2008 Best & Brightest" list and in Thames&Hudson's selection of "60 innovators" shaping our creative future. In 2010 Blueprint Magazine included him as one of the "25 People Who Will Change the World of Design", Forbes listed him as one of the "Names You Need To Know" in 2011 and Fast Company named him as one of the "50 Most Influential Designers in America". He was also featured in Wired Magazine's "Smart List 2012: 50 people who will change the world". His Digital Water Pavilion at the 2008 World Expo was hailed by Time Magazine as one of the "Best Inventions of the Year". In 2012 Carlo was selected with his design office as one of the top three young architects for the "Premio Fondazione Renzo Piano".

Carlo has been a presenter at TED 2011, program director at the Strelka Institute for Media, Architecture and Design in Moscow, curator of the 2012 BMW Guggenheim Pavilion in Berlin, and was named Inaugural Innovator in Residence by the Queensland Government. The Italian Minister of Culture also named Carlo as a member of the Italian Design Council — an advisory board to the Italian Government that includes 25 leaders of design in Italy. He is currently serving as a member of the World Economic Forum Global Agenda Council for Urban Management and is a curator for the Future Food District Pavilion for Expo 2015 in Milan.

Charles C. Hugo Landscape Design

Charles C. Hugo Landscape Design is New England's premier landscape design build firm that goes beyond transforming the outdoors within the traditional boundaries of the landscape designer. Creating new and exciting as well as functional and aesthetic design elements drives the studio to achieve new standards of beauty, form and structure that provide solutions and satisfaction. From vertical gardens to traditional gardens native New England shrubs, trees and perennials are intentionally utilized to create spaces that once completed seem to have always existed. While plants add grace, color and texture they are always in balance with the existing environment. Garden designs are executed in conjunction with the site's current architectural elements as well as newly proposed elements such as screened porches, decks and other structures. Natural stone is used to create terraces for entertaining, walls for sitting and delineating boundaries, and walkways and natural stone steps that connect outdoor features and people — all elements are fully integrated thus creating perfect spaces. Each aspect of the process, from design conception to implementation and management, to post plant care and bed maintenance are managed in-house and with great attention to detail.

Charles (Chuck) Hugo has been designing and building beautiful landscapes on New England's seacoast for over two decades. With his background in the aesthetics of design and the principals of engineering and construction he is uniquely qualified to bring creative and practical solutions to his clients' concerns and bring the full spectrum of his art and craft to the resolution of his projects.

Cherem Arquitectos

Cherem, *arqs*

Cherem Arquitectos is an architectural firm based on Mexico City, its work is focused on a way to approach each project, and to solve the fundamental problems in a particular way, solving space, proportion, light and materials. The firm sees an importance on exploring the materials and the use of them in each project. They are not focused on a specific set of stylistic mannerisms, they see each project as a different oportunity to create something unique.

Their early commissions include a Hotel and Hostel

from Grupo Habita on a Historic Palace on Downtown Mexico, a house for a Mexican soccer player, a store for Marika Vera lengerie, subsequent projects have ranged of scales and different typologies from interior to mixed used buildings.

D&M

D&M will enhance the look and feel of any home. Our pure materials, natural colours and classy shapes and forms confirm the power of simplicity and harmony in any interior. Cosy living into the smallest detail is what our three company brands are all about:

D&M depot — Everything you need to create a highly personal interior decor that exudes an air of classy luxury; ceramics, glass, large pots, wicker baskets, tealights, wood, tastefully designed accessories for the home.

D&M fabrics — Natural, carefully selected fabrics fashioned into beautiful cushions and plaids.

D&M table — Crockery to create an hospitable and attractive-looking table for everyday use and those special occasions: plates, bowls, cups, etc.

Fábio Galeazzo

Know for joining together beauty and sustainability, Fábio Galeazzo works with timelessness.

Creative in everything he proposes, he mixes materials with colors in a feisty and fearless way. Being know for a professional that don't repeat himself, his work has soul, where the past and the comtemporary live together in total harmony. He plays with the diachrony completely free and this is one of the trademarks of his language. Reread the time in the objects and the objects of time with his own style.

In 2004, founded Galeazzo Design interior design and product development, with a young and aligned team, being awarded nationally and internationally. His work is gaining prominence among the international press and it's been published in more than 50 countries.

Farmery

The Farmery is an innovative urban market and farm designed to produce and sell locally made food. The Farmery combines a retail grocery and indoor agricultural systems that raise the value of food by offering the customer an educational and stimulating food shopping experiee. At the Farmery, the consumer can witness and participate in the growth and harvest of crops and fish.

The Farmery currently has 2 production prototypes in Clayton, NC, where it has developed its unique growing systems. The Farmery team also has a retail prototype in front of Burt's Bees headquarters at American Tobacco Campus in downtown Durham, NC. The retail prototype is a 20 ft shipping container covered in living walls, except the windows and doors. The Farmery team grows watercress, lettuce and herbs inside the container and allows customers to grab a bag and harvest their own crops, mimicking the experience of the much larger full-scale version of the Farmery.

Fytogreen

"Green roofs and vertical gardens help the world re-invest in its natural beauty. We grow gardens to please the eye, to please the soul, to challenge the elements and challenge our spirit. We share the magic of watching gardens grow on buildings within our cities, for the joy of our whole community."

Started 2002, Fytogreen is now Australia's leading specialist in design and constructing gardens on built structures. With hundreds of completed projects around Australia our research and garden designs focus on Ecological Sustainability to ensure all our gardens survive for the natural life of the plants.

Green Studios

Along with Beirut city taking back its position as the cultural and art hub of the Arab world, and in an effort from developer Solidere to bring in the latest green technologies into the city center, a couple of projects that include vertical landscape interventions were proposed early in 2009 by award winning French architectural firm "Moatti-Riviere".

Green Studios who had just patented its advanced hydroponic version of the green wall, was awarded the design development and execution of a series of installation in the middle of Beirut Souks_Solidere. This green wall system mimics the structure and functions of a human body; it has a solid structure (the body) on which the whole green wall is based, a skin, a core element (heart) pumping nutrition and water, in addition to the control board (brain) that regulates and monitors it.

Greenworks AB Sweden

Greenworks constantly sees new needs for indoor plantings and therefore it develops new items to meet that demand. Significant for Greenworks products is the central role of the plants with its capacities: air purification, humidification and oxygenation of the air, sound absorption, aesthetic expression, enforcement of the green profile of your brand.

Plant walls have many positive consequences. The combination of substrate, plants and trapped layers of air in the plant wall system act as a good sound insulation. Sound waves are captured and reflected. The substrate blocks lower sound waves, whilst plants obstruct higher frequencies. A plant surface keeps your office quieter and creates more pleasant surroundings.

A plant wall in your indoor set muffles noise, and the sound quality in its surroundings is less hollow. The amount of sound insulation differs per plant and also depends on how densely the plant wall is built up. Many studies have demonstrated the soothing and relaxing psychological effect of greenery. Walking through botanical gardens reduces blood pressure and lowers the heart beat. Another study shows that the presence of greenery helps one recover more quickly from stress. So looking out on a plant wall is good for your health!

Hofman Dujardin Achitects

Hofman Dujardin Architects, founded in 1999, is an office specialised in Architecture, Interior and Product design. The office is located at the waterfront in the centre of Amsterdam. Hofman Dujardin Architects is working on a wide variety of architectural, interior and product designs with a fabulous team of twenty architects and interior designers. Our main goal is to create inspiring buildings, interiors and products that enhance life at large. A surrounding in which people can live and work in an optimized way and where the investments made are fully effected. For office buildings we design creative working environments in which the employees can work efficiently and get inspired continuously. Condominiums and dwellings we transform into interiors with maximum comfort and fully adjusted to ideas and wishes of the clients. And by executing product designs such as the Bloomframe balcony, we express our relentless effort to innovate, surprise and challenge.

i29 | interior architects

We are i29 | interior architects, a creative and versatile interior design studio. Our aim is to create intelligent designs and striking images. Space is the leitmotiv, the result is always clear, with a keen eye for detail. Our approach is practical yet based on strong ideas articulated in clear concepts. We try to get to the core of things but keep it looking simple. Our clients are open minded and involved. It is most important to us to enjoy the process together and to get everything out of it!

We are not alone in our voyage. In a short period of time many projects have been realized for a wide variety of clients, both private and business. We've been nominated and won several awards like the Rotterdam Design Award, Dutch Design Award, LAI Award and The Great Indoors Award. We won the Dutch Design Prize for best interior design and The Great Indoors Award for best office design. Projects have been published in (inter) national magazines and books. Our core team of designers, extended by a growing network of freelance specialists work closely together to create interesting and unexpected ideas.

Founders: i29 | interior architects: jaspar Jansen & Jeroen Dellensen

Jardins de Babylone

Jardins de Babylone is a company founded in 2004 by Amaury Gallon. Pioneer in plant walls, Amaury Gallon filed a patent in 2007 on a 100% synthetic fiber made from recycled, he quickly created new concepts from vegetal. Amaury Gallon was inspired by organic or natural vegetated form a space, scenography, an object, a piece of furniture, to reconcile man to nature. Jardins de Babylone meets the needs of architects, decorators, builders on their problems of vegetalisation whether a plant wall, planted design, garden or terrace or maintenance of green walls.

The company is a design office wich conceived, built maintenance in his creations whether indoor or outdoor. For projects tailored and creative Jardins de Babylone is based on these patents, know-how and knowledge of botany. Our creations bring an extraordinary differentiated picture, sublimating your projects.

The company will adapt to your style plant project, so that it becomes part of the overall design of the development. It realizes projects conscientious, unique to meet your needs and those of your customers, and has a unique know-how rare modernizing its field of activity.

LIN inc.

"LIN" is a distinctive Japanese word often used to describe dignified woman, who is not flamboyant but nevertheless whose presence stands out. We aim our designs to evoke the same atmosphere like "LIN".

Atsushi Suzuki worked for OUT. DeSIGN CO., LTD. as a designer, and was appointed to extensive projects from retail shops to office interior design.

In 2003, he set up his own practice LIN currently specializing in retail design.

Lango Hansen Landscape Architects

Lango Hansen Landscape Architects (LHLA) provides a wide range of services in landscape architecture, planning, and urban design. Over the past nineteen years, the firm's principals have successfully designed public parks, urban plazas, school and university campuses, corporate headquarters, private residences, and public facilities.

LHLA approaches each project as a unique opportunity to develop designs that address the particular character of the site, the specifics of the program, and the needs of individuals and communities. Using a variety of media, such as models, sketches, and computer-aided tools, the firm explores integrated design solutions. With a commitment to detail and craftsmanship, LHLA creates long-lasting designs that express the innate character and value of each landscape.

Metropole Architects

Metropole Architects was founded in 1997 by Nigel Tarboton. Tyrone Reardon joined the office in 2002, and became a partner in 2004. We are based in Durban, Kwa-Zulu Natal, South Africa.

The majority of our current and completed work is upmarket residential. A significant portion of these projects have been in luxury estates such as Zimbali Forest and Golf Estates (Ballito), Simbithi Golf and Eco Estates (Ballito), Izinga Ridge Estate (Umhlanga), Nkwazi Ridge (Zinkwazi), Kirtlington equestrian estate (Hillcrest), Cotswold Downs Golf Estate (Hillcrest) and Imbabala Forest Estate (Pennington).

We also currently have a number of commercial, industrial and public buildings in the design stage.

Meyer + Silberberg Land Architects

MEYER + SILBERBERG LAND ARCHITECTS

Meyer + Silberberg's collaborative design studio is based in Berkeley, California. They are a team of dedicated professionals passionate about the design of the landscape. David Meyer and Ramsey Silberberg have taken great care to shape their practice into a uniquely responsive and personable enterprise. Coming from some of the most admired practices in the country, they bring over 40 years of knowledge and experience to every project. Meyer + Silberberg serves a wide range of clients, including non-profit institutions, private developers, academic campuses, business associations, and government agencies. What unites the work is the premise that there is always something inherent in a site and the surrounding culture that wants to be expressed. So they express it with distinction and with simplicity. They craft landscapes that transcend and anchor themselves in the hearts and heads of the people who use them.

Meyer + Silberberg is recognized internationally for the increasingly rare ability to transform a great idea into an exceptional physical space. The firm does this through passionate engagement with their clients, tireless exploration and refinement of design, and a renowned reputation for construction and execution.

Paisajismo Urbano

paisajismo urbano

In light of the growth of our cities and the limited space for gardens planning, Paisajismo Urbano is a Company dedicated to the design of vertical gardens and characterized for having a green mentality. This Green philosophy originates from the passion for nature and its growing; and the will to reduce the effect of the lack of horizontal space for gardens in the cities.

The work of Ignacio Solano, expert in biology and founder of Paisajismo Urbano; and his extensive research in rainforests of all around the world over the recent years, are the basis of observation and study of interspecific processes between flora and microfauna common in the rainforest areas.

The philosophy of Paisajismo Urbano, is to invest their revenues in research. They constantly move to forest and natural sites around the world, looking for new plants species, developing new substrates, taking measurements and improving techniques for the developing of vertical gardens. All this has resulted in bringing the concept of vertical gardens one step further, creating what Ignacio Solano termed as Vertical Ecosystems, result of applied biology.

As specialists in design and creation of vertical garden systems, we strongly believe that a city with natural spaces is more attractive and is highly beneficial for both environment and citizens. Our Vertical Ecosystem interacts with people's everyday life, we are trying to give color to gray cities and eliminate pollution and stress. Our designs for facades, roofs and terraces are the lungs which will refresh and purify oxygen around us.

Patrick Blanc

Born on June 3rd, 1953 in Paris.

Education :

Docteur de 3ème cycle (1978), Université Pierre et Marie Curie, Paris 6

Docteur d'Etat ès Sciences (1989), Université Pierre et Marie Curie, Paris 6

Work situation :

Scientist for CNRS (Centre National de la Recherche Scientifique) since 1982

Prizes :

Award winner, French Science Society, Botany, 1993

Award winner, Innovation Contest, 1999. Ministère de la Recherche

Talent d'or 2002 du Sommet du Luxe et de la Création

Virgile prize for the book *Etre Plante à l'ombre des forêts tropicales*, 2003

Chevalier de l'Ordre des Arts et des Lettres, 2005

Silver medal, Architecture Academy, 2005

One of 50 Best Inventions of the Year, Time Magazine, 2009

RIBA Honorary Fellowship (Royal Institute of British Architects), 2010

Patrick Nadeau

Patrick Nadeau graduated in architecture and design. Supported by the National Centre for Plastic Arts and invited in 1998 to stay at the Villa Kujoyama in Kyoto by the French Ministry of Foreign Affairs, he began to be particularly interested in plant design.

In 1999, Patrick Nadeau set up his own consultancy in Paris and developed projects that combine elements of architecture, design and nature. This unique approach has attracted the support of innovative companies and institutions such as Authentics, Boffi, la Maison Hermès, Kenzo Parfums, Louis Vuitton.

His personal exhibition untitled "Nature Individuelle" (2010) and a book writed by Thierry de Beaumont Patrick Nadeau / Végétal design (Alternatives and Particule14 editions, 2012) illustrates his approach.

Patrick Nadeau also acts as a director of research at the ESAD in Reims where he creates "plants design" workshop. He is also diploma supervisor at the Ecole Camondo (Les Arts Décoratifs) in Paris.

PAUL CREMOUX Studio

PAUL CREMOUX Studio is an architectural firm committed to distinguished sustainable eco-effective building designs. Our goal is to produce architecture that celebrates life, enriches the natural environmental and the human spirit. We envision a process that is integrated by a concept that balances environment enrichment proposals, beauty and social responsibility with the client's needs and desires.

PAUL CREMOUX Studio work has been exhibited at Mexico's City Museum of Modern Art, (MAM), the Royal Institute of British Architects (RIBA), London UK. Mexico's City Public spaces and galleries. Winners and Finalists in several international contests like, Best 30 Houses of the World at (WAN) World Architectural News, or Second Won Place for the Guadalajara Library International Contest. We are holders of several grants and scholarships like the CONACYT (The National Council of Science and Technology) and FONCA (The National Fund for Culture and Arts) among others, We impart academic courses at the UNAM (National Autonomous University of Mexico), IBERO (Universidad Iberoamericana) Anahuac University, and ITESM (The Monterrey Institute of Technology and Higher Education). Media recognition includes work publish at diverse design national and international magazines, TV show interviews, Books, Newspapers and design architectural web blogs.

PUSHAK AS

PUSHAK AS was founded as a joint-stock company in 2008. The partners Camilla Langeland, Sissil Morseth gromholt, Marthe Melbye and Gyda Drage Kleiva have worked together on architectural assignments since 2002.

In the last century, Architecture has forgotten how to adapt to climate, and hence to the human body. This has lead to environment that are unpleasant to be in, and buildings that use too much energy. By considering wind and sun, more comfort can be achieved with less recourses; this is the credo for both the tiny boxes on the beach in Finnmark and our urban housing developments.

PUSHAKs portfolio of built work includes homes, rest stops, a crematorium and a kindergarten. Currently four more homes are under construction. PUSHAK's most important work has been won in design competitions: Vestfold Crematorium, Moss your City at the Architecture Foundation, Rommen Sustainable Housing and the Gateways to Sjunkhatten National Park.

RA \\ ARCHITECTURAL & DESIGN STUDIO

RA \\ ARCHITECTURAL & DESIGN STUDIO, has its main office in Lisbon, Portugal.

The practice works internationally on cultural, commercial and residential projects providing masterplanning, architecture, interior design, product and furniture design services for both the private and public sectors. The practice is currently working in several projects worldwide such as Angola, Brasil, Montenegro, Belgium and France.

Two essential components have always dominated the work developed by RA \\ ARCHITECTURAL & DESIGN STUDIO: the client and respect for the scenery.

As a matter of fact, the efficiency of this atelier is continuously expressed in the conciliation of both components. Architecture is a multi-subject activity in which technical sophistication and cost management are essential. Yet, architecture is simultaneously an art, and this must never be forgotten.

Our capacity to join together all of these attributes as well as to perform in accordance to the principal of good professionalism has resulted in over a decade of fully accomplished projects.

In a moment of such rapid and intense globalization, where the true basis of our activity are so often forgotten, we strive to further implement and strengthen our presence. Thus, we've extended the activities of RA \\ ARCHITECTURAL & DESIGN STUDIO to the areas of Urban Planning and Real Estate Promotion. These significant and growing variants of activities have been developed either alone or with a number of strategic partners.

sufficient detail

RaStenia

RaStenia is a 100% Russian company designing, mounting and maintaining interior plantwalls since 2008. RaStenia Plantwalls, or fytowalls, are tailored individually to fit perfectly the inner structure and architecture of the interior.

These vertical gardens are fully accomodated to the harsh and at times unpredictable North-West and Central Russian climate conditions, including lack of natural light, availability and quality of flowers and other factors.

Nowadays RaStenia living walls come with full or partial automation, vary in size and floral design, integrate easily into the space. We have offices in Moscow and St. Petersburg, and operate throughout Russia.

Distinguishing features of RaStenia fytowalls are as follows:

•Flexibility in forms and finishing materials,

•Custom design,

•Large choice of plants to select from (40+ species),

•Easy integration with smart house systems,

•Proved compliancy with international ecological standards and pronounced ecological policy supported by the "Vitality Leaf" ecolabel.

Ricardo Marinho

Ricardo Marinho Paisagismo Ltd., since 1982, is a Studio-Office, located in Fortaleza, BRAZIL, led by the Landscape Architect/Artist, Ricardo Marinho, specialized in refined and detailed landscape projects, panels, murals and automatic irrigation systems.

Internationally recognized, has won an Award as Landscape Architect of the year in 1994, in São Paulo, Brazil, granted by A&D Magazine. His projects are designed as art work, and vary in scale and scope from parks, squares, private residences, resorts, hotels and environmental planning.

His designs easily convert into places where one can rest, play, gather socially and enjoy the pleasure of the senses.

Roel de Boer

Roel de Boer is a designer (graduated from Design Academy Eindhoven in 2010) that strives for sustainable solutions in both social and environmental sense. Although starting from "big issues", his work has a very personal and sensitive quality to it, both through its aesthetics, being a result of his hands-on approach, as through its concepts that come out of an intuitive reflection on the contemporary world and society.

In his designs, de Boer brings people to nature and nature to people. Contrasts between urban and natural (living) environments are a fascination that form a red thread throughout his projects. Being born at an island, life in the city with its vibrancy and social diversity made de Boer think about the meaning of "home" and the way environment affects people in their personal lives. According to de Boer, the ultimate living environment would combine, although sometimes contradicting, qualities of both the quietness and isolation of nature and the socially dense and interactive city.

De Boer explores both worlds as a "beach comber". In this way he collects inspiration and experiences as well as materials, shapes and colours. As a result his work shows both natural elements and man-made constructions, in this way it reflects again the fascination of the duality between raw, organic nature and the refined, colourful and complex city with its many impulses.

RSP ARCHITECTS PLANNERS & ENGINEERS (PTE) LTD.

RSP is one of the largest and most established architectural and engineering professional practices in Singapore. Together with associates, it provides comprehensive professional building consultancy services in architecture, planning, urban design, civil & structural and mechanical & electrical engineering and interior design.

RSP has offices in China, Vietnam, the UAE, UK and Ghana, with combined group staff strength exceeding 800. RSP has undertaken an extensive portfolio of projects across many development types ranging from residential, commercial, institutional, and office developments to key infrastructure projects. RSP's expertise has been independently recognized in the many awards granted to both our completed developments and to the firm for outstanding professional excellence.

Somdoon Architects

Somdoon Architects

Somdoon Architects is a team of Architects lead by Punpong Wiwatkul and Puiphai Khunawat. Our strategy is to gather and study all relevant information of each project to generate the architectural ideas. We then select the ideas with most potential to develop further and repeatedly refine them in multi architectural scales to achieve the best design solution. We believe that good architecture can be achieved from good design and professional commitment. We explore problems, offer unique design solutions and monitor the implementation with the clients and consultants because we believe that every process is equally important to achieve the exceptional standard.

Somdoon Architects is now being involved in various scale and types of projects ranging from residential high rise, low rise, hotel, office and retail. We have been published in the international architectural publications and have won awards including WAF (World Architecture Festival) Award, International Property Award and MIPIM Asia Award.

Prior to launching Somdoon Architects, Punpong and Puiphai practiced in an international firm in Singapore for 8 years where they were associate architects for award winning high rise projects. They have lectured in universities and polytechnic in Thailand and Singapore. They also served as judges in the architectural competitions.

SpY

SpY is an urban artist whose first endeavors date back to the mid-eighties. Shortly after, already a national reference as a graffiti artist, he started to explore other forms of artistic communication in the street. His work involves the appropriate urban elements through transformation or replication, commentary on urban reality, and the interference in its communicative codes.

The bulk of his production stems from the observation

of the city and an appreciation of its components, not as inert elements but as a palette of materials overflowing with possibilities. His ludic spirit, careful attention to the context of each piece, and a not invasive, constructive attitude, unmistakably characterize his interventions.

SpY's pieces want to be a parenthesis in the automated inertia of the urban dweller. They are pinches of intention, hidden in a corner for whoever wants to let himself be surprised. Filled with equal parts of irony and positive humor, they appear to raise a smile, incite reflection, and to favor an enlightened conscience.

Thomas Corbasson, Karine Chartier

"All our projects spring from a total absence of preconceived desires, a willingness to explore what ought to be where. Our role is that of a catalyst: a project is a slow-maturing process that leads eventually to the logic of everything from appropriate design to a correct choice of materials and a resolution of each detail, something far beyond the straitjacket of 'standards' and other bureaucratic headaches. Such is the price of giving birth to a passion…"

2013 — Dejean Price delivered by Architecture Academy.

Work nominated for the European Union Prize Mies van der Rohe Award 2013.

2012 — Silver medal to the CIO / IAKS AWARD.

2011 — Prize-winner of the Prize list sustainable revelations of the CAUE 80.

2010 — General public price of Contemporary Architectures of the Parisian metropolis for the housings in the marais.

2008 — Selected for the Venice Biennale, to be exhibited in the French Pavilion.

2005 — Winners of the Prix Européen Bauwelt de la première oeuvre architecturale for the "Maison de l'architecture" at the Récollets Convent in Paris.

2002 — Winners of the "Nouveaux Albums de la Jeune Architecture" award.

1999 — The agency is set up

Tierra Design (S) Pte Ltd.

Tierra Design (S) Pte Ltd. is a multidisciplinary design firm established in 1995 in Singapore by Franklin Po. As designers with a focused desire to explore the relationship of the arts, culture, nature and land, we provide professional design services in architecture, landscape architecture, interior design, master planning, urban design and sustainable environmental design, in order to enhance the quality of life for people who occupy the spaces that we create.

Tierra projects are known for their economy of planting and sensual natural simplicity, beauty and quiet reserve. Faithful to these origins, Tierra depends heavily on the natural rhythms and hues of the earth, incorporating materials, colours and sounds into integrated spaces. We have been the recipient of a number of awards for design excellence. Our projects include prestigious residential, commercial, hospitality and institutional projects in Singapore, Malaysia, Indonesia, India, China and Abu Dhabi.

We embrace diversity in our people, with collaboration playing a vital role in creating our unique, thoughtful and holistic designs. Our aim is to help clients make intelligent and well-informed decisions to enhance value for them and create a better future for our planet.

Verde360°

Verde360° is a Mexico City based design firm that specialises in living walls for urban environments. The firm was founded in 2006 by Yael Ehrenberg Hellion, Francis Vermonden, and Jacques Vermonden.

Their multidisciplinary team designs and builds high quality custom made vertical gardens in a city cluttered

with buildings and full of bare walls, but with a rich environment of young architects and urban designers conscious and in need of using these spaces in different ways.

Thanks to their inspiration and creative professions, the studio of Verde360° has created around 7, 000 m² of stunning living walls for important clients and innovative architects. Yael lived and worked in Kenia, East Africa, South of England and San Francisco, California besides other countries in Europe. She brought with her a dynamic portafolio of ideas inspired by the landscapes of these countries, by the innovative ideas of greening up the cities and her experience working with plants as an agronomic engineer and landscape designer. On the other hand, Francis, the younger of the three, was about to finish his studies in industrial design and the subject of his thesis was a green wall system. So he had the time and perseverance to search for material with a criteria that it should be recyclable and produced in Mexico in order for Verde360° to head towards a sustainable direction. Jacques, a Belgium citizen born and raised in the Congo complemented the team with his vast experience as an architect , and integrated the language necessary to consolidate the infrastructure of their living walls in the design concept of the buildings.

tres birds workshop

tres birds workshop is a full-service architecture and general contracting firm based in Denver, Colorado. Our primary objective is to unite humans with natural systems through the built environment.

The natural world runs on highly sophisticated and efficient systems that create balance and order. We seek to mimic this efficiency and view each project as a total system to be approached in an entirely integrated and holistic manner, using cross-disciplines: art, science (biology, ecology), anthropology, architecture and construction management.

From historical renovations and commercial retrofits to new construction, from dynamic office space and creative studios to retail and mixed-use development, from single family homes to multi-unit residential buildings, from civic engagement to private, non-profit and public sectors, from temporary installations to permanent fixtures, locally, domestically or abroad: our goal is to work on projects with people who share values of environmental stewardship, human health, community enrichment and artistic appreciation.

Vo Trong Nghia Architects

Vo Trong Nghia Architects

Founded in 2006, Vo Trong Nghia Architects is a leading architecture design office in Vietnam. The offices are located in Ho Chi Minh City and Hanoi, where more than 30 international architects, engineers and staffs work closely on cultural, residential and commercial projects. Currently, Vo Trong Nghia Architects undertakes projects in Vietnam, China, Cambodia and Mexico.

The company explores new ways to create green architecture for the 21st century, experimenting the possibilities of natural energy such as light, wind and water, by using natural and local materials while maintaining the essence of Asian architectural expression and contemporary design vocabulary.

The bamboo projects represent the company's endeavor in pursuing green architecture embedded in an eco-environment. Bamboo is an environmentally friendly material with outstanding reproductive ability, echoing the spirit of Asian culture toward the nature. Thanks to bamboo's attributes of small and uneven dimension as well as high flexural capacity, we are able to construct curving structure to maximize its potential and cultivate its grace of curvature.

Along the same spirit, other company's projects in public and residential buildings are green in the nature, collegial in the local community, and sustainable in the environment. While the usage of inexpensive local materials expresses regionality and collegiality with the local community, the application of natural energy and greenery represents the company's effort towards a sustainable environment.

VRTIŠKA • ŽÁK

Roman Vrtiška and Vladimír Žák have met already during AAAD studies, where they started their collaboration. Both spent their internships at Alvar Aalto Univeristy in Helsinki, Finland, where they received Awards for their work. After graduating at AAAD Prague, they became a part of the new and fresh generation of Czech designers with wide range of interests and a highly professional approach. Since then, they have been working on different projects from architecture, product design to graphic design field. They have been working for such clients as: Adidas, Belda Factory, Česká spořitelna, Diesel,

Egoé, Heineken, Interspar, Jitona, Moravské sklárny Květná, Indeco, Inno, mmcité, Ruukki, Scandium, Spokar, Tammi, Tereza Maxová, Teroforma, UP závody, Verreum, etc.

Wayward Plants

waywardplants

Wayward Plants is a chartered landscape architecture practice based in London — an award-winning collective of designers, artists and urban growers. We create imaginative landscapes that explore social exchange and botanical narratives. Our projects include the acclaimed Union Street Urban Orchard (2010), the Urban Physic Garden (2011), and recently, the Queen's Walk Window Gardens (2013), transforming the most activated space in London into 80m of community allotments, and visited by an estimated 8 million people.

Wayward Plants takes a unique approach to landscape through the creation of narrative environments. Our projects express stories that connect people through nature, producing vibrant spaces that are productive, meaningful and imaginative. Our work extends beyond design to project delivery, creative direction, event curation and community design and build workshops. At the heart of our projects are large - scale plant exchanges that bring people together through plants and their stories.

Woolly Pocket

woollypocket

Pockets were first invented out of a personal need for a simple, DIY-consumer friendly system for gardening vertically, not yet available on the market. With Miguel's background as a sculptor and Rodney's background in manufacturing, they invented the breathable Woolly Pockets with internal moisture control that are made from recycled plastic bottles in USA. Now, the Nelson brothers are turning the gardening industry down side up. And the Woolly Pocket family is also helping millions of students learn nutrition and gardening through their Woolly School Garden program by creating a living garden classroom for students K-12.

ARTPOWER

Acknowledgements
We would like to thank all the designers and companies who made significant contributions to the compilation of this book. Without them, this project would not have been possible. We would also like to thank many others whose names did not appear on the credits, but made specific input and support for the project from beginning to end.

Future Editions
If you would like to contribute to the next edition of Artpower, please email us your details to: artpower@artpower.com.cn